REVCO'S
Freezer Cookery

By Margaret Deeds Murphy

Dorison House Publishers, Inc., New York

ABOUT THE AUTHOR

Margaret Deeds Murphy, author and Home Economist, was born in Strombsburg, Nebraska, received her Home Economics degree from the University of Nebraska in 1937, and has been cooking, testing, and writing about food ever since. She is the author of several cookbooks, has been associate food editor of Woman's Home Companion magazine, and was the head of the Recipe Test Kitchen of General Foods Corporation. Maggie Murphy lives with her husband on Cape Cod, where she operates a test kitchen for the development of recipes. She is currently preparing the food pages for Gray's Sporting Journal.

Copyright © 1976 by Dorison House Publishers, Inc.

Published by Dorison House Publishers, Inc.

183 Madison Avenue, New York, N.Y. 10016

ISBN: 0-916752-02-X

Library of Congress Catalog Number: 76-407-28

Manufactured in the United States of America

TABLE OF CONTENTS

Using Your Freezer

Your Revco-built freezer will be one of the most useful and important pieces of equipment in your home once you have learned to use it so that it best suits the needs of your family. A trip through your local supermarket freezer section will give you an idea of the array of foods which can be frozen. Some you may not want to duplicate at home, others will be welcomed to your freezer. In any event, the vast variety will let you know at once that many choices will have to be made when planning foods for your own freezer.

Have a Buying Plan

Just because someone is having a sale on pork chops, do not fill your freezer so full of pork chops that you cannot take advantage of the next week's steak sale. Plan how you wish to use the freezer space to suit your family's needs best. Impulse buying for your freezer can turn into disaster for your food budget. Even if your buying plan is casual, it will be better than none.

Organize Food in the Freezer

Whether you have an upright or a chest type freezer, store similar foods in the same area of the freezer. Have a section for meats, one for vegetables, another for fruits, breads, desserts, etc. In this way you will have some idea of your inventory. The other way is to keep an inventory list on the outside of the door and actually check things in and out. While this is ideal, it can become tedious and out of hand when many family members use the freezer.

Filling the Freezer the Most Efficient Way

For families with gardens or nearby fresh garden produce stands, freezing their own vegetables "from scratch" may be the best and least expensive method. For people who have access only to vegetables in grocery stores, it may be equally good and less expensive to buy commercially frozen vegetables and store in your freezer ready for home use. Decisions like this should be made in all categories of food. Your time is valuable. Is it more efficient for you to trim and package meats for the freezer or to pay a few cents more per pound to have your butcher do it? Do you have a neighborhood bakery whose bread and rolls are superb? You can buy and freeze to save trips to the baker. How much help can you get from family members in preparation of food for the freezer? These and many similar questions can be asked and answered in filling your refrigerator most efficiently.

The main purpose of owning a freezer is to give you a wide choice of foods at your finger tips any hour of the day or night at a saving in time and money.

The following general freezing directions are designed to help you get the most efficient usage of your freezer.
- Freeze the best. Freeze only foods of high quality.
- Freeze correct quantities. Your freezer is designed to freeze approximately 3 pounds per cubic foot freezer capacity at one time. If larger quantities than this are to be frozen, store the excess in the fresh food compartment of your refrigerator until the first quantity is frozen. In plain English this means don't put too much food to be frozen in the

freezer at one time. The faster food becomes frozen the better its quality is retained. This is why all food to be frozen should be WELL chilled before it goes into the freezer. It allows the food to freeze more rapidly and does not lower the overall temperature of the freezer any appreciable number of degrees.

- To freeze quickly, place packages flat against refrigerated surfaces of freezing area. After packages are frozen solidly, they may be rearranged and stacked. Then new food to be frozen can be put in the freezer.

- Store commercially frozen food immediately any place in the Food Freezer. Make the trip from the store freezer department to the home food freezer as fast as possible so no thawing occurs.

REFREEZING

Occasionally, frozen foods are partially or completely thawed before it is discovered that the freezer is not operating.

The basis for safety in refreezing foods is the temperature at which thawed foods have been held and the length of time they were held after thawing.

You may safely refreeze frozen foods that have thawed if they still contain ice crystals or if they are still cold—about 40° F.—and have been held no longer than 1 or 2 days at refrigerator temperature after thawing. In general, if a food is safe to eat, it is safe to refreeze.

Even partial thawing and refreezing reduce quality of fruits and vegetables. Foods that have been frozen and thawed require the same care as foods that have never been frozen. Use refrozen foods as soon as possible to save as much of their eating quality as you can.

—Reprinted from Home and Garden Bulletin No. 10
U.S. Department of Agriculture

IF A POWER OUTAGE OCCURS—
WHAT TO DO WITH THE FREEZER

Should a power outage occur, first find out how long it is going to last. If power will be restored within 24 hours, you should not have too many worries.

In a large, full freezer which is kept shut as much as possible, foods will stay frozen up to 48 hours. In a smaller freezer or a partially loaded freezer, 24 hours is the limit.

Do these things:

First try to find out how long the emergency is apt to last. If it is an electrical breakdown, see if you can borrow a freezer from the repair company or dealer until yours is repaired, particularly if it is to be longer than 24 hours before your own facilities will be usable. Or if there is a local freezer-locker plant, see if you can rent temporary facilities for storage of the frozen food. In transporting it to the freezer-locker, wrap the frozen food heavily in newspapers.

Instruct members of the family NOT to open the freezer. If you need to get things out if it, plan your needs and take them all out at the same time and as quickly as possible to conserve the cold air inside the freezer.

Do not put any non-frozen items in the freezer during this period.

Continue to eat the foods from the freezer. As long as the temperature remains below 40° F. the food is being adequately protected.

Foods which have ice crystals in them can be refrozen without worry. Remember to expect a loss of quality when it is necessary to refreeze frozen foods. It might even be wise to mark the packages with this information in planning for their future use.

If the power outage has occurred while you are on vacation so that it is impossible to tell how long the situation has been in effect, your nose will be your best judge as to whether or not to keep the food. If there is ANY doubt, discard it.

Selecting Freezer Packaging Material

Once you've purchased your freezer, you are on your way to year 'round savings on the food bill and the pleasure of eating freezer-fresh foods out of season. You will be able to bring out whole meals put in the freezer for use on days when you are too busy with other activities to cook.

But you have to cooperate in two ways to get the optimum use of your freezer. One, as has already been mentioned, is to freeze only the best food available; the other to package it properly for the freezer.

Unless you are very certain of the kinds of foods you wish to freeze, it might be well to wait until you are into your freezing program before buying great quantities of freezer packaging material. For example, most poultry and meats do not require freezer containers, so if you've purchased a quantity of freezer containers and end up freezing a lot of poultry and meat, you may be stuck with containers not needed.

The purpose of packaging materials is to keep food from losing moisture and to protect the color, flavor and nutritive value of the foods. For these reasons all food should be packaged in moisture-proof, vapor-proof packaging materials and the words "freezer wrap" or "freezer container" or a similar statement should be displayed prominently on the box in which it is purchased.

If food is improperly packaged, the dry air in the freezer will rob moisture from the food and leave the food with dry spotted areas, called freezer burn. Packaging and wrapping should fit tightly to prevent an excess accumulation of frost inside the airspace in the package.

Satisfactory packaging for freezing should be moisture-, vapor-, and leakproof. It must protect foods from giving off or absorbing odors, and should not impart a flavor to the food nor absorb grease, oil or water. It must be durable.

Packaging is classified as rigid and nonrigid.

Rigid Containers

This classification includes glass, tin, aluminum, plastics or waxed fiberboard. These containers can be used for fruit and vegetables and for liquid packs. All rigid containers, including glass, should be straight sided. Most rigid containers can be reused.

Nonrigid Containers

Nonrigid containers include a variety of packaging materials such as moisture/vapor-resistant aluminum foil, pliofilm, cellophane and various types of laminated papers. These materials are made up in sheets or bags and are suitable for both liquid or dry packs. The filled bags may be inserted in outer cardboard boxes as a protection for the food and an aid to stacking. These flexible packaging materials can be used for meats, poultry, fish, baked goods and other foods of irregular shape. Freezer tape or twists are used to insure a tight seal.

The most efficient size of package to use is that which holds an amount to serve your family for one meal. This avoids left-overs and waste.

Filling and Sealing Containers and Other Useful Information

Rigid containers made of plastic and fiberboard have enough resiliency that they can be filled almost to the top. Glass containers, particularly when used for a product with a high liquid content, should always have a head space for expansion of frozen products. In pint jars it should be ½-inch, in quart jars 1-inch. There are straight sided glass jars especially manufactured for freezing and/or canning. But straight sided peanut butter or other similar jars can be washed out and used for freezing. Never use left over cottage cheese cartons or other containers from products purchased from the refrigerated case. They are not designed for freezing. However, plastic containers left from a product purchased in the freezer section may, as a rule, be re-used for freezing.

If there is any question about the tightness of a lid, cover the top of the jar with plastic wrap and then put on the lid or put freezer tape around the edge of the cover. The lids for straight sided freezing/canning jars, as long as they are not bent, may be re-used for freezing though they cannot in canning.

Occasionally when products are to be stored for long periods of time, it is wise to cover the wrapped package with stockinette. This is a knitted cotton stretch tube which protects from breaks which might occur when the packages are shifted in the freezer.

In using nonrigid packaging material — always fill bags as full as possible and seal carefully with the twists provided (or rubber bands) excluding all air, or if using seal-a-bag equipment (which comes with its own bags) seal as directed.

When wrapping foods, wrap as closely as possible. Protect sharp bones with several thicknesses of foil or plastic wrap. The "drug store" wrap which brings the two long sides up together and then folds under until a tight wrap is secured is preferred. (See illustration) Seal with freezer tape. Masking tape makes an excellent tape, and costs less than freezer tape.

From time to time you will find references to "tray pack" freezing. This is when the food is spread out uncovered on trays and frozen as quickly as possible. Immediately upon being frozen it is packaged in family size amounts in freezer bags or containers. The advantage of tray pack freezing is to have individually frozen foods rather than blocks. It is especially useful for vegetables but can be used for single servings of meat.

DRUG STORE WRAP

1. Place the food in the center of the wrapping paper.
2. Bring the two opposite sides of the sheet together.
3. Fold in lock seam until the last fold is tightly fitted on the food.
4. Press the wrapping snugly against the food.
5. Fold the ends into points excluding as much air as possible.
6. Bring the ends up and seal with tape or tie securely.

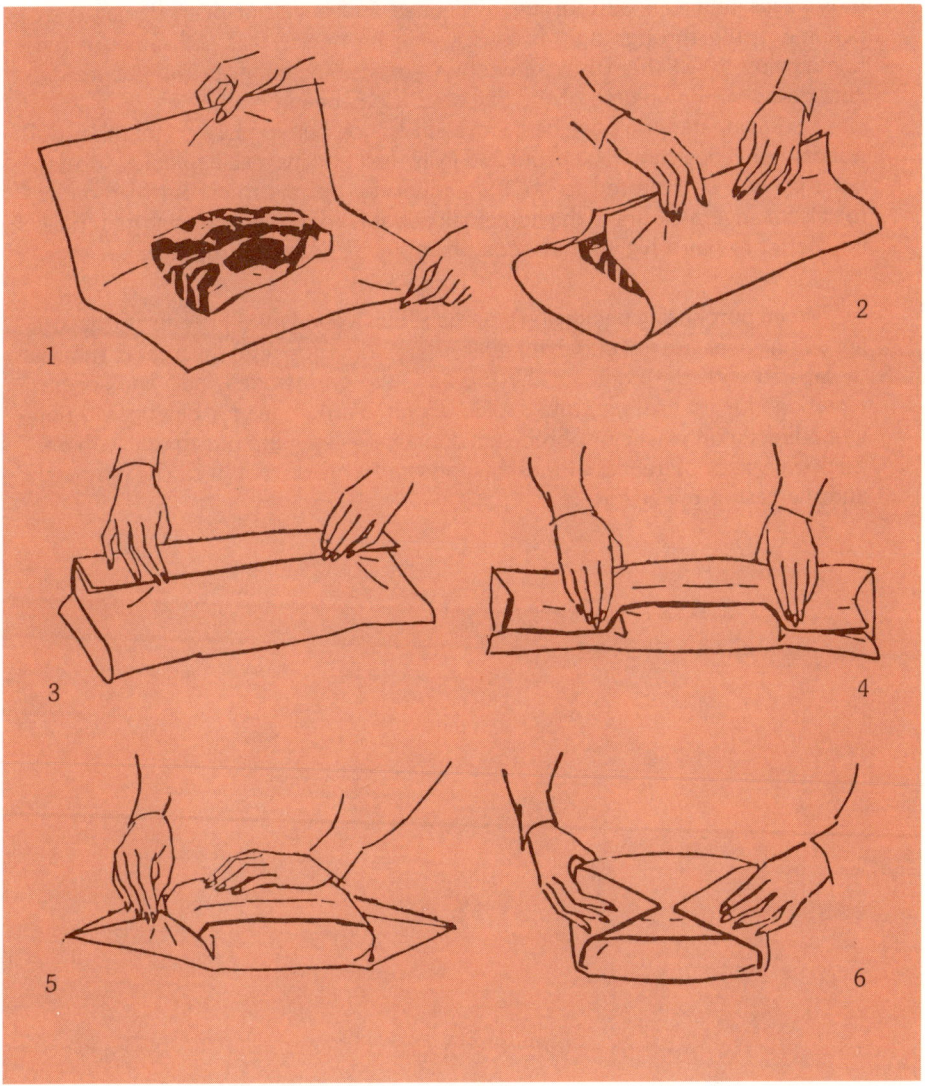

Re-use of Packaging Materials

Most rigid containers can be reused for freezing. When tin cans that require a sealer have been used it is necessary that they be reflanged before sealing again. Tin cans with slip-top closures, glass jars, plastic and other rigid containers are reusable while aluminum foil boxes are not well adapted for reuse because of the type of folding seal. Cardboard cartons (fiberboard) are reusable if they are plastic or wax lined, and if the lining is not damaged or dirty. The folding paperboard cartons used to protect the inner bag may be reused as can those bags that can be thoroughly cleaned and have not been damaged or become brittle through age. If bags are to be reused it is advisable for the homemaker to seal them using either twists or a rubber band, as the heat-sealing cuts down on the volume of the bag after it has been opened.

Packaging materials are best stored in a cool, humid place so that they do not dry out. They should be protected from dust and insects. If materials do dry out they can be restored to good condition by placing them between damp towels for several hours. If the homemaker wants to reuse packaging materials, it is better to pay a higher initial cost than buy a cheap non-reusable package.

Labeling Foods for the Freezer

When purchasing packaging materials, buy a good marking pen. (Ordinary felt writing pens are not suitable.) Everything which goes into the freezer should be labeled with the name of the product, the date frozen, and any special directions for its use, i.e., raw cookie dough, instructions for baking. Do not write directly on plastic or fibreboard containers if one intends to re-use them. Stick on a piece of freezer or masking tape and write on that. It can be removed and the carton relabeled.

Meats, Poultry, Fish and Shellfish

MEATS, POULTRY, FISH AND SHELLFISH

MEATS

Freezing is one of the most practical ways of preserving meats. The meats to be frozen should be carefully selected and frozen immediately in the proper packaging. Frozen meats should always be stored at 0°F. or below.

How to's With Meat

- Freeze family size packages to avoid left-overs and perhaps wasted meat. Label each package with kind and type of product number of servings and cooking method.
- Chops, meat patties, thin steaks or similar single serving portions can be layered with several thicknesses of wax or parchment paper before overwrapping. Or tray freeze, unwrapped. When frozen, immediately pack into freezer bags and label, date.
- Freeze meats quickly. Turn the temperature control in the freezer to lowest setting to hasten freezing and prevent other products in the freezer from warming up.
- Unless it has been specially packaged by the butcher, meat, as it is purchased, is not suitably wrapped for the freezer. Since meat has a limited storage life in the refrigerator, it is not wise to buy great quantities when time is not available to wrap and freeze it within one or two days.
- If it is necessary to trim fat and bone from meat before cooking, it is more practical to do so before freezing. In the case of beef, the beef suet may be frozen to feed to the birds in the winter. The bones may be packaged and frozen to make beef stock later. Remember, too, that pork, ham, lamb and veal bones are all good additions to the stock pot.
- Ground beef may be cooked lightly in a skillet until the red is just gone, fat drained off, cooled and frozen in containers. Defrost to use for spaghetti sauce, Spanish rice, Sloppy Joe's or other dishes requiring ground beef cooked in this matter. One pint equals approximately 1 pound cooked beef.
- Save preparation time by packaging ground beef in the form in which it will be used, i.e., meat patties, meat loaf, bulk for top stove cooking.
- When freezing patties, pull out a long sheet of freezer paper, arrange beef patties on the paper at intervals, cut between with a scissors and wrap.
- Remove all bones possible from meat. It saves up to 35% of storage room in freezer.
- Freeze steaks flat, not folded. They will take up less room and defrost more quickly.
- Do not add unnecessary salt to meat before freezing. It hastens rancidity.
- Before planning a freezing session, check supplies.

Meats to Freeze and Storage Time

Fresh Meats

	In freezer at 0° F.
Roasts (Beef and Lamb)	6 to 12 months
Roasts (Pork and Veal)	4 to 8 months
Steaks (Beef)	6 to 12 months
Chops (Lamb)	6 to 9 months
Chops (Pork)	3 to 4 months
Ground and Stew Meats	2 to 3 months
Variety Meats (Liver, etc.)	3 to 4 months
Sausage (Pork)	2 to 3 months

Processed Meats

Bacon	1 month
Frankfurters	2 weeks
Ham (Whole)	1 to 2 months
Ham (Half)	1 to 2 months
Ham (Slices)	1 to 2 months

Cooked Meats

Cooked Meats and Meat Dishes	2 to 3 months
Gravy and Meat Broth	2 to 3 months

Note: It is not recommended to freeze luncheon meats or smoked sausage or dry or semi-dry sausage.

If you have an opportunity to buy meat by the whole, half or quarter, here are some tips:

- Be certain that an experienced meat cutter is available. Even a quarter of an animal is no job for an amateur.
- Most commercial freezer-locker operations have experienced meat cutters who can both cut and package bulk meat purchases. They have, as well, temporary storage space if there is too much meat for your own freezer at the time.
- If you do the cutting at home have refrigerator space to chill wrapped meat well before freezing. Since 3 pounds per cubic foot of total storage space is the maximum to be frozen at one time, both refrigerator and freezer space should be available.
- In calculating the saving cost when buying bulk meat, here are some yield charts. Remember also, that the grade of beef governs the cost per pound. A lesser (cheaper) grade might be satisfactory for pot roasts, stew meat and ground beef, but not for steaks or roasts.

Approximate yields of trimmed beef cuts from animal with a carcass weight of 420 pounds (live weight, 750 pounds).

Steaks and oven roasts	172 pounds ...	40 percent
Pot roasts	83 pounds ...	20 percent
Stew and ground meat	83 pounds ...	20 percent
Total	338 pounds ...	80 percent

So in calculating the cost of the beef, add 20 percent to the original cost since that is the loss in cutting.

Approximate yields of trimmed beef cuts from a dressed forequarter weighing 218 pounds.

Steaks and oven roast	55 pounds ...	25 percent
Pot roasts	70 pounds ...	32 percent
Stew and ground meat	59 pounds ...	37 percent
Total	184 pounds ...	84 percent

In this case, the loss in cutting is 16 percent, so that would be added to the original cost.

Approximate yields of trimmed beef cuts from dressed hindquarters weighing 202 pounds.

Steaks and oven roast	117 pounds ...	58 percent
Stew, ground meat, and pot roasts	37 pounds ...	18 percent
Total	154 pounds ...	76 percent

The loss is higher here, being 24 percent but there is a much greater proportion of steaks and oven roasts in this portion of the beef.

Approximate yields of trimmed pork cuts from a hog with a carcass weight of 176 pounds (live weight, 225 pounds).

Fresh hams, shoulders, bacons, jowls	90 pounds ...	50 percent
Loins, ribs, sausage	34 pounds ...	20 percent
Total	124 pounds ...	70 percent
Lard rendered ...	12 pounds ...	27 percent

By making lard, there is a much larger recovery from pork.

Approximate yields of trimmed lamb cuts from a lamb with a carcass weight of 41 pounds (live weight, 85 pounds).

Legs, chops, shoulders	31 pounds ...	75 percent
Breast and stew meat	7 pounds ...	15 percent
Total	38 pounds ...	90 percent

The recovery on lamb is 90 percent, which is very good.

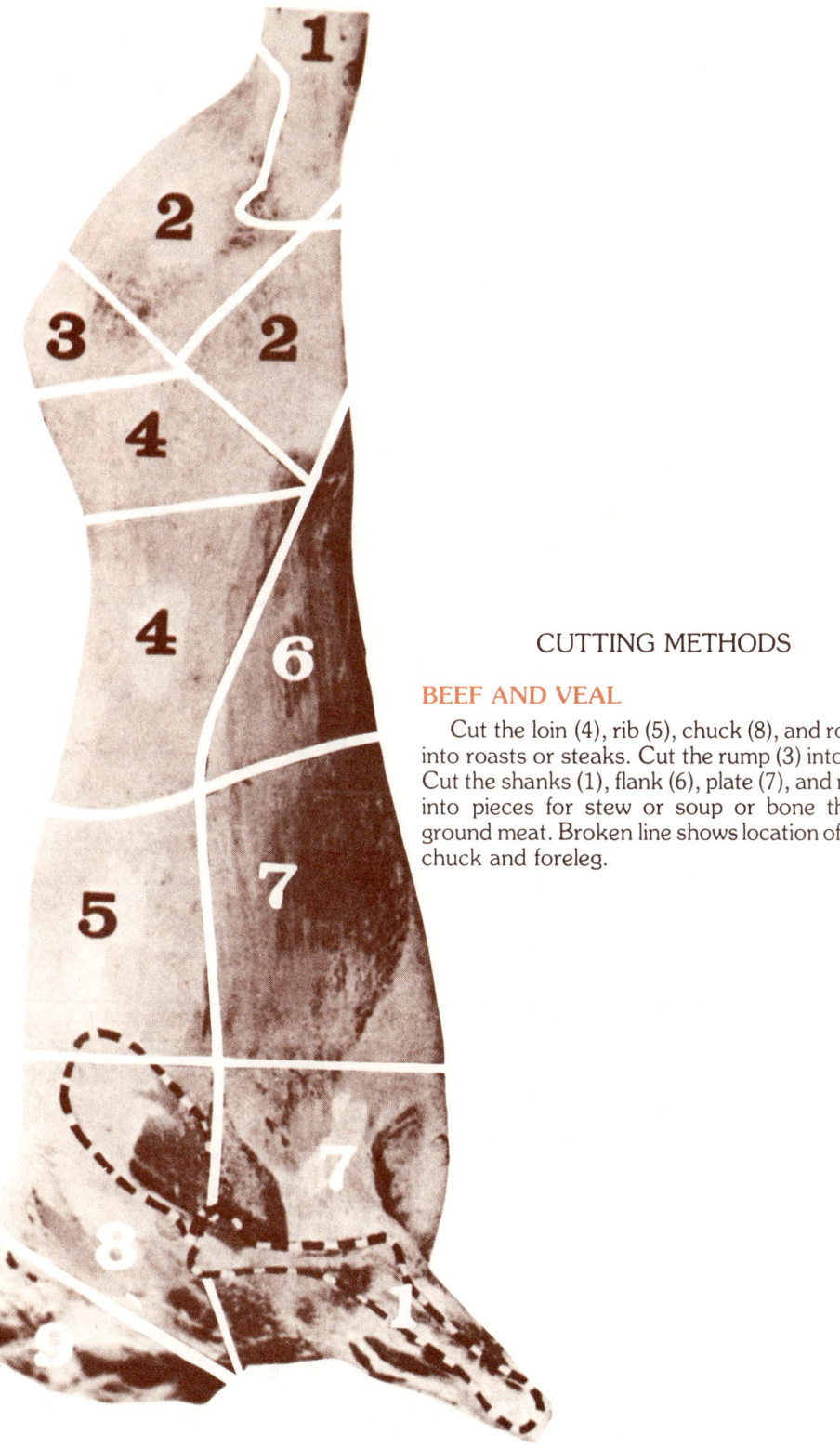

CUTTING METHODS

BEEF AND VEAL

Cut the loin (4), rib (5), chuck (8), and round (2) into roasts or steaks. Cut the rump (3) into roasts. Cut the shanks (1), flank (6), plate (7), and neck (9) into pieces for stew or soup or bone them for ground meat. Broken line shows location of bone in chuck and foreleg.

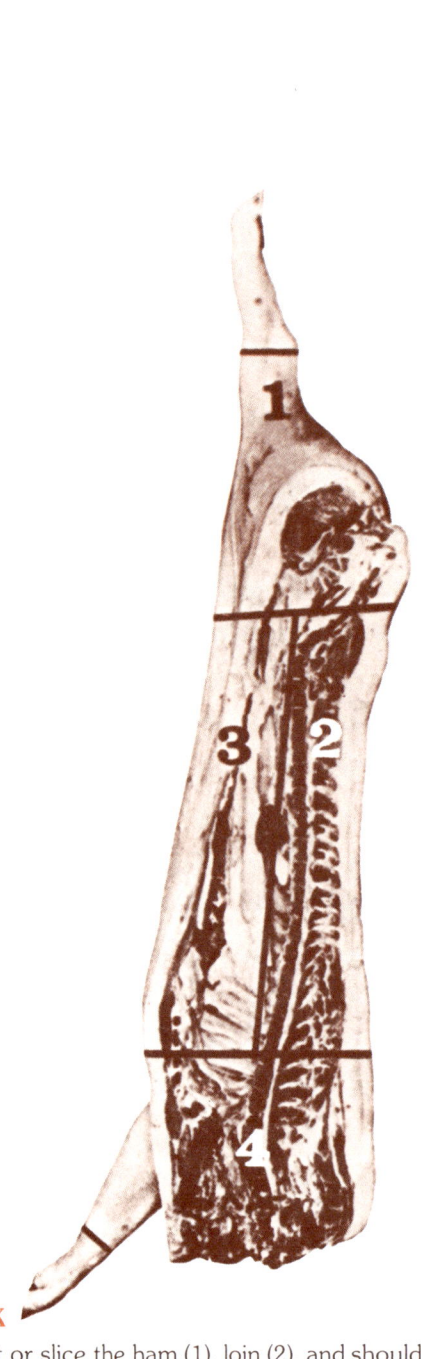

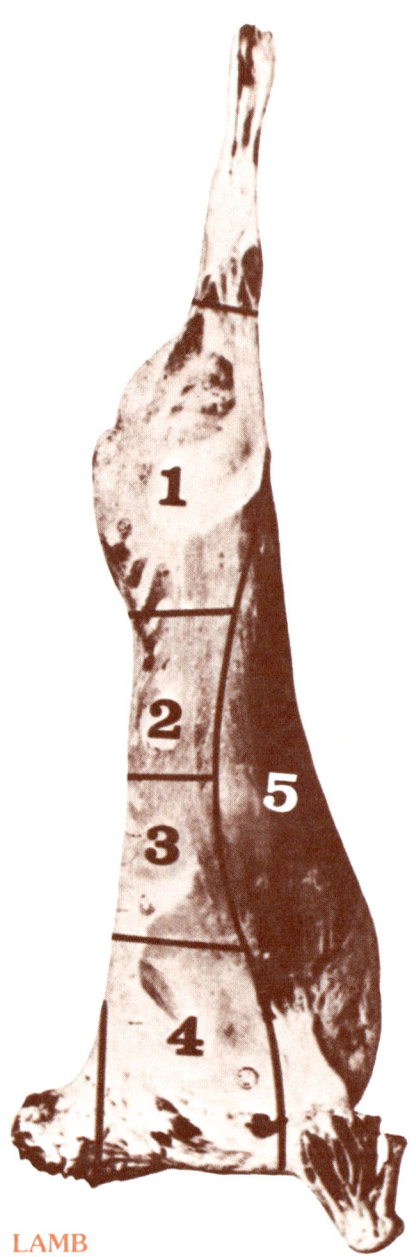

PORK

Cut or slice the ham (1), loin (2), and shoulder (4) into roasts, steaks, or chops. Trim the thin bacon strip (3) for curing, or cut into boiling pieces. Trim all meat closely, using lean for sausage and fat for lard.

LAMB

Trim the legs (1) and shoulders (4) into uniform-sized roasts; cut rib (3) and loin (2) into chops; bone breast (5), shanks, and neck for stew or ground lamb.

BEEF CHART

RETAIL CUTS OF BEEF — WHERE THEY COME FROM AND HOW TO COOK THEM

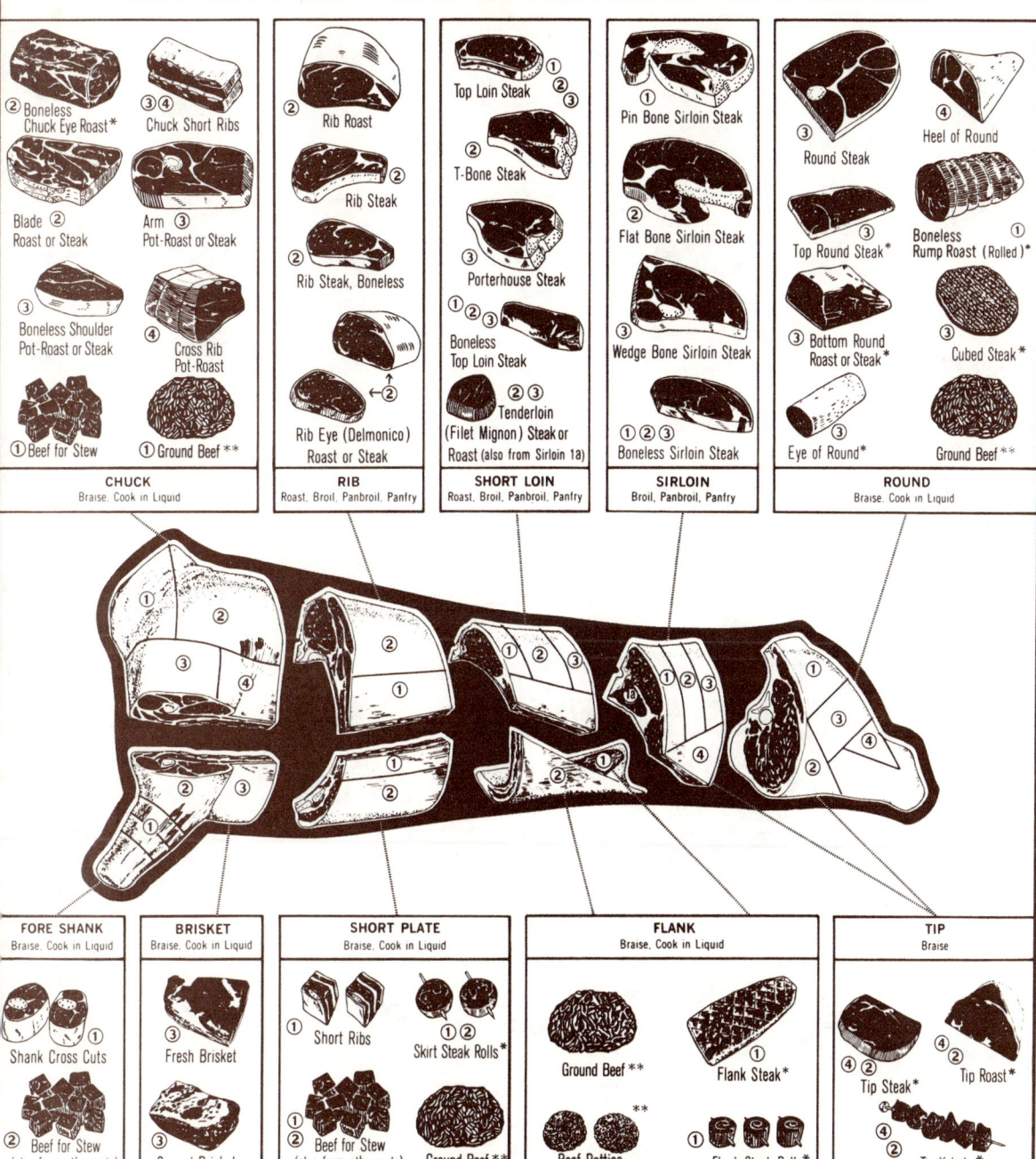

CHUCK
Braise, Cook in Liquid

- ② Boneless Chuck Eye Roast *
- ③④ Chuck Short Ribs
- Blade ② Roast or Steak
- Arm ② Pot-Roast or Steak
- ③ Boneless Shoulder Pot-Roast or Steak
- ④ Cross Rib Pot-Roast
- ① Beef for Stew
- ① Ground Beef **

RIB
Roast, Broil, Panbroil, Panfry

- ② Rib Roast
- ② Rib Steak
- ② Rib Steak, Boneless
- ② Rib Eye (Delmonico) Roast or Steak

SHORT LOIN
Roast, Broil, Panbroil, Panfry

- ①②③ Top Loin Steak
- ① T-Bone Steak
- ③ Porterhouse Steak
- ①②③ Boneless Top Loin Steak
- ②③ Tenderloin (Filet Mignon) Steak or Roast (also from Sirloin 1a)

SIRLOIN
Broil, Panbroil, Panfry

- ① Pin Bone Sirloin Steak
- ② Flat Bone Sirloin Steak
- Wedge Bone Sirloin Steak
- ①②③ Boneless Sirloin Steak

ROUND
Braise, Cook in Liquid

- ③ Round Steak
- ④ Heel of Round
- ③ Top Round Steak *
- ① Boneless Rump Roast (Rolled) *
- ③ Bottom Round Roast or Steak *
- ③ Cubed Steak *
- ③ Eye of Round *
- ③ Ground Beef **

FORE SHANK
Braise, Cook in Liquid

- ① Shank Cross Cuts
- ② Beef for Stew (also from other cuts)

BRISKET
Braise, Cook in Liquid

- ③ Fresh Brisket
- ③ Corned Brisket

SHORT PLATE
Braise, Cook in Liquid

- ① Short Ribs
- ①② Skirt Steak Rolls *
- ② Beef for Stew (also from other cuts)
- ① Ground Beef **

FLANK
Braise, Cook in Liquid

- Ground Beef **
- ① Flank Steak *
- ** Beef Patties
- ① Flank Steak Rolls *

TIP
Braise

- ④② Tip Steak *
- ④② Tip Roast *
- ④② Tip Kabobs *

* May be Roasted, Broiled, Panbroiled or Panfried from high quality beef.
* May be Roasted, (Baked), Broiled, Panbroiled or Panfried.

This chart approved by
National Live Stock and Meat Board

© National Live Stock and Meat Board

PORK CHART

RETAIL CUTS OF PORK — WHERE THEY COME FROM AND HOW TO COOK THEM

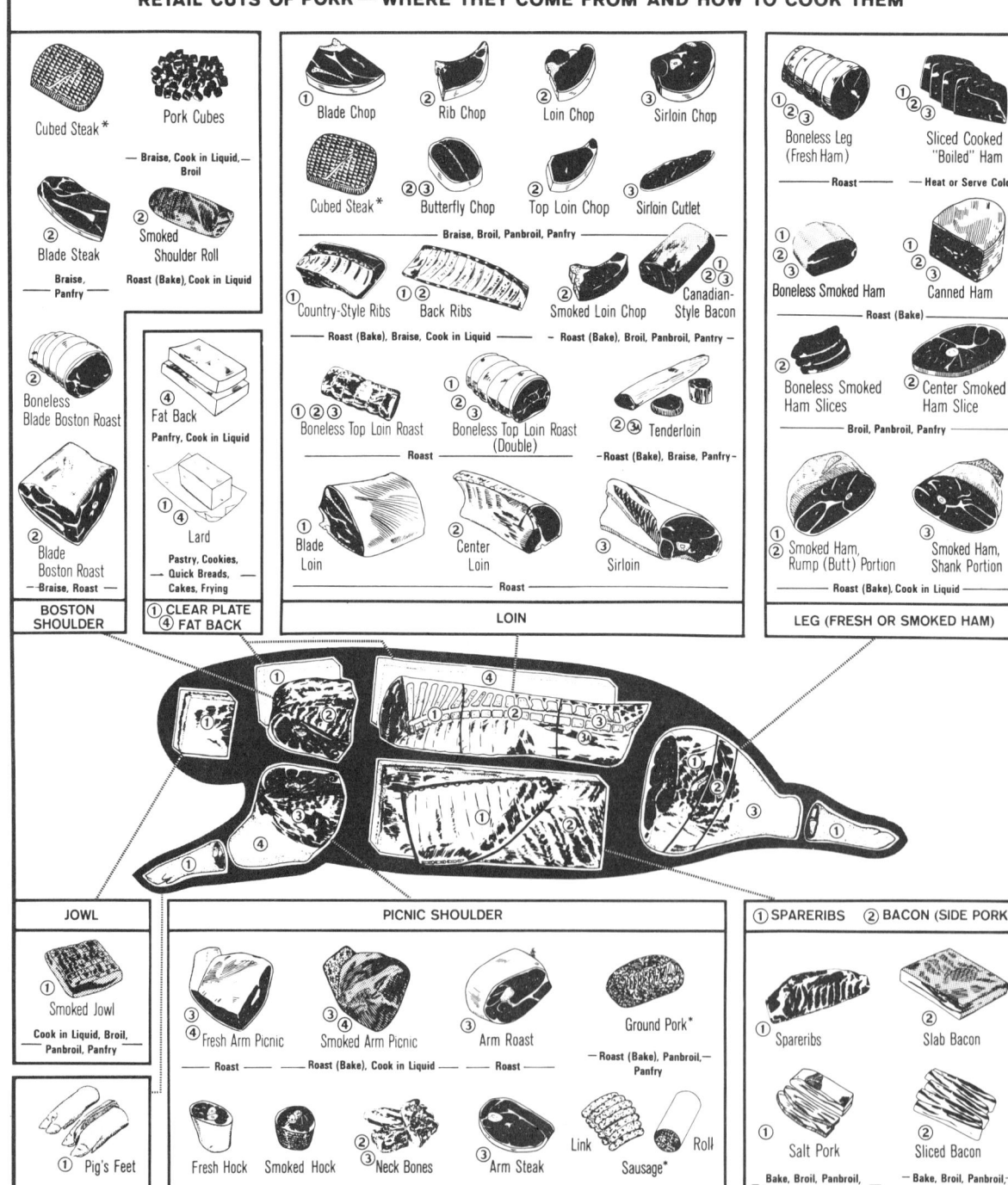

BOSTON SHOULDER

Cubed Steak*

Pork Cubes

— Braise, Cook in Liquid, — Broil

② Blade Steak

Braise, Panfry

② Smoked Shoulder Roll

Roast (Bake), Cook in Liquid

② Boneless Blade Boston Roast

② Blade Boston Roast

— Braise, Roast —

① CLEAR PLATE ④ FAT BACK

④ Fat Back

Panfry, Cook in Liquid

① ④ Lard

Pastry, Cookies, Quick Breads, Cakes, Frying

LOIN

① Blade Chop

② Rib Chop

② Loin Chop

③ Sirloin Chop

Cubed Steak*

② ③ Butterfly Chop

Top Loin Chop

Sirloin Cutlet

— Braise, Broil, Panbroil, Panfry —

① Country-Style Ribs

① ② Back Ribs

Smoked Loin Chop

② ③ Canadian-Style Bacon

— Roast (Bake), Braise, Cook in Liquid — — Roast (Bake), Broil, Panbroil, Pantry —

① ② ③ Boneless Top Loin Roast

① ② ③ Boneless Top Loin Roast (Double)

② ③ Tenderloin

— Roast — — Roast (Bake), Braise, Pantry —

① Blade Loin

② Center Loin

③ Sirloin

— Roast —

LEG (FRESH OR SMOKED HAM)

① ② ③ Boneless Leg (Fresh Ham)

① ② ③ Sliced Cooked "Boiled" Ham

— Roast — — Heat or Serve Cold —

① ② ③ Boneless Smoked Ham

① ② ③ Canned Ham

— Roast (Bake) —

② Boneless Smoked Ham Slices

② Center Smoked Ham Slice

— Broil, Panbroil, Pantry —

① ② Smoked Ham, Rump (Butt) Portion

③ Smoked Ham, Shank Portion

— Roast (Bake), Cook in Liquid —

JOWL

① Smoked Jowl

Cook in Liquid, Broil, Panbroil, Panfry

① Pig's Feet

— Cook in Liquid, Braise —

PICNIC SHOULDER

④ Fresh Arm Picnic

Smoked Arm Picnic

③ Arm Roast

Ground Pork*

— Roast — — Roast (Bake), Cook in Liquid — — Roast — — Roast (Bake), Panbroil, — Panfry

Fresh Hock

Smoked Hock

② ③ Neck Bones

③ Arm Steak

Link / Roll Sausage*

— Braise, Cook in Liquid — — Cook in Liquid — — Braise, Panfry — — Panfry, Braise, Bake —

① SPARERIBS ② BACON (SIDE PORK)

① Spareribs

② Slab Bacon

① Salt Pork

② Sliced Bacon

— Bake, Broil, Panbroil, Panfry, Cook in Liquid — — Bake, Broil, Panbroil, — Panfry

*May be made from Boston Shoulder, Picnic Shoulder, Loin or Leg.

This chart approved by
National Live Stock and Meat Board

© National Live Stock and Meat Board

LAMB CHART

RETAIL CUTS OF LAMB — WHERE THEY COME FROM AND HOW TO COOK THEM

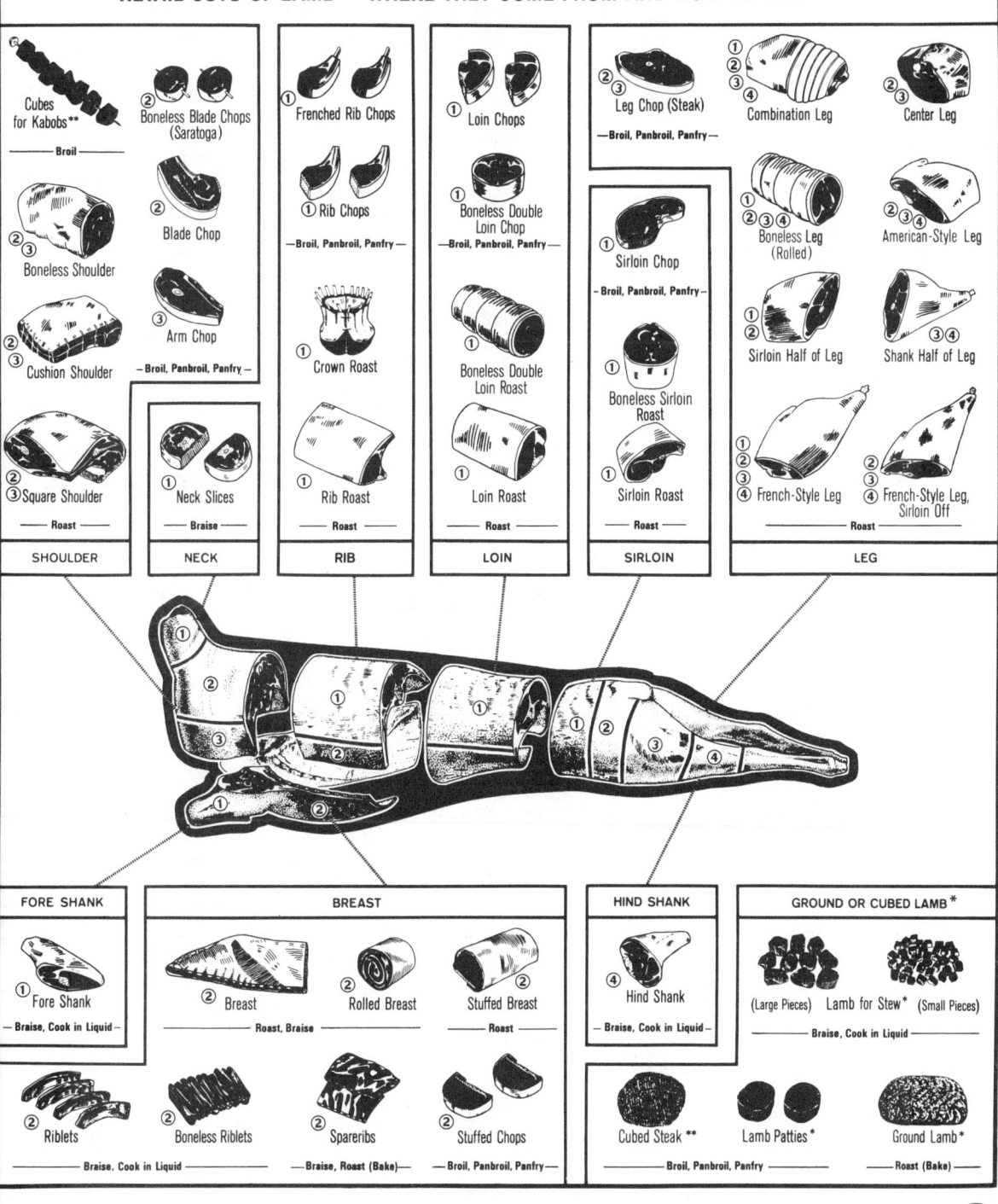

SHOULDER

- Cubes for Kabobs **
- — Broil —
- ② Boneless Blade Chops (Saratoga)
- ② Blade Chop
- ③ Arm Chop
- — Broil, Panbroil, Panfry —
- ②③ Boneless Shoulder
- ②③ Cushion Shoulder
- ②③ Square Shoulder
- — Roast —

NECK

- ① Neck Slices
- — Braise —

RIB

- ① Frenched Rib Chops
- ① Rib Chops
- — Broil, Panbroil, Panfry —
- ① Crown Roast
- ① Rib Roast
- — Roast —

LOIN

- ① Loin Chops
- ① Boneless Double Loin Chop
- — Broil, Panbroil, Panfry —
- ① Boneless Double Loin Roast
- ① Loin Roast
- — Roast —

SIRLOIN

- ③ Leg Chop (Steak)
- — Broil, Panbroil, Panfry —
- ① Sirloin Chop
- — Broil, Panbroil, Panfry —
- ① Boneless Sirloin Roast
- ① Sirloin Roast
- — Roast —

LEG

- ①②④ Combination Leg
- ②③ Center Leg
- ①②③④ Boneless Leg (Rolled)
- ②③④ American-Style Leg
- ①② Sirloin Half of Leg
- ③④ Shank Half of Leg
- ①②③④ French-Style Leg
- ②③④ French-Style Leg, Sirloin Off
- — Roast —

FORE SHANK

- ① Fore Shank
- — Braise, Cook in Liquid —

BREAST

- ② Breast
- ② Rolled Breast
- ② Stuffed Breast
- — Roast, Braise —
- — Roast —
- ② Riblets
- ② Boneless Riblets
- ② Spareribs
- ② Stuffed Chops
- — Braise, Cook in Liquid —
- — Braise, Roast (Bake) —
- — Broil, Panbroil, Panfry —

HIND SHANK

- ④ Hind Shank
- — Braise, Cook in Liquid —

GROUND OR CUBED LAMB *

- (Large Pieces) Lamb for Stew* (Small Pieces)
- — Braise, Cook in Liquid —
- Cubed Steak **
- Lamb Patties *
- Ground Lamb *
- — Broil, Panbroil, Panfry —
- — Roast (Bake) —

Lamb for stew or grinding may be made from any cut.
*Kabobs or cube steaks may be made from any thick solid piece of boneless Lamb.

This chart approved by
National Live Stock and Meat Board

© National Live Stock and Meat Board

VEAL CHART

RETAIL CUTS OF VEAL — WHERE THEY COME FROM AND HOW TO COOK THEM

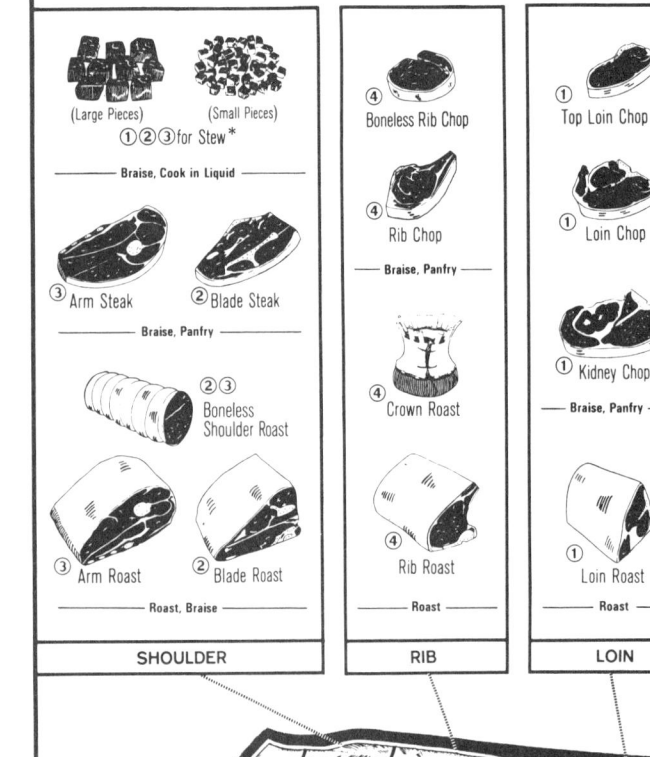

SHOULDER

(Large Pieces)   (Small Pieces)
① ② ③ for Stew*

— Braise, Cook in Liquid —

③ Arm Steak   ② Blade Steak

— Braise, Panfry —

② ③ Boneless Shoulder Roast

③ Arm Roast   ② Blade Roast

— Roast, Braise —

RIB

④ Boneless Rib Chop

④ Rib Chop

— Braise, Panfry —

④ Crown Roast

④ Rib Roast

— Roast —

LOIN

① Top Loin Chop

① Loin Chop

— Braise, Panfry —

① Kidney Chop

— Braise, Panfry —

① Loin Roast

— Roast —

SIRLOIN

Cubed Steak **

① Sirloin Chop

— Braise, Panfry —

① Boneless Sirloin Roast

① Sirloin Roast

— Roast —

ROUND (LEG)

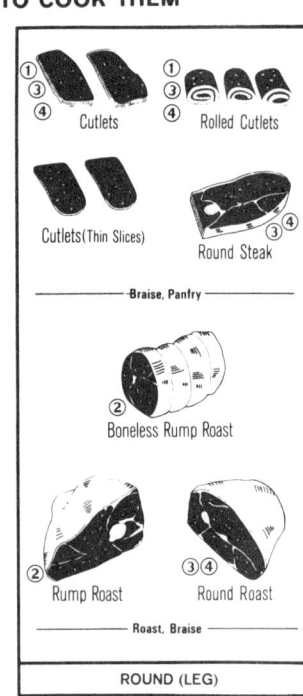

① ③ Cutlets   ① ③ ④ Rolled Cutlets

Cutlets (Thin Slices)   ③ ④ Round Steak

— Braise, Panfry —

② Boneless Rump Roast

② Rump Roast   ③ ④ Round Roast

— Roast, Braise —

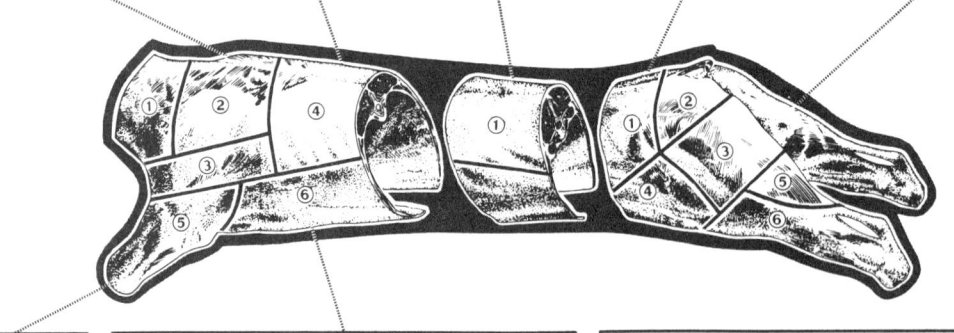

SHANK

⑤ Shank

⑤ Shank Cross Cuts

Braise, Cook in Liquid —

BREAST

⑥ Breast

⑥ Stuffed Breast

— Roast, Braise —

⑥ Riblets   ⑥ Boneless Riblets   ⑥ Stuffed Chops

— Braise, Cook in Liquid —   — Braise, Panfry —

VEAL FOR GRINDING OR CUBING

Rolled Cube Steaks **   Ground Veal*   Patties*

— Braise —   — Roast (Bake) Braise, Panfry —

Mock Chicken Legs*   * City Chicken   Choplets*

— Braise, Panfry —

*Veal for stew or grinding may be made from any cut.

**Cube steaks may be made from any thick solid piece of boneless veal.

This chart approved by
National Live Stock and Meat Board

© National Live Stock and Meat Board

20   Meats

Defrosting and Cooking Frozen Meats

Meats may be cooked frozen or defrosted. If cooked frozen allow 20 to 50 percent more time for cooking than if defrosted. (The latter, larger figure is for large cuts.)

Defrosting can be done in the original packaging in the refrigerator. If the package is waterproof it may be defrosted in cold water. Most Microwave ovens give directions for electronic defrosting.

When defrosting in the refrigerator allow several hours or overnight depending on the size of the meat being defrosted.

Roasting Meat

Any tender cut of beef, lamb, pork or veal may be roasted. Defrost completely before cooking or add roasting time as indicated.

Season with salt and freshly ground pepper. Place on rack in an open roaster with fat side up. Insert a meat thermometer so that it is in the center of the largest muscle. Be sure that it does not touch bone.

Roast at 325° F. to 350° F. Roast to desired degree of doneness as indicated on thermometer.

If no thermometer is used, follow these timetables.

Standing Beef Ribs

2 ribs .... rare .... 33 minutes per pound
2 ribs .... medium .... 43 minutes per pound
2 ribs .... well done .... 50 minutes per pound

Lamb Leg .... 30-35 minutes per pound
Pork Loin .... 35-40 minutes per pound

Always cook pork well done

Veal Leg .... 25 minutes per pound

PORK CERVANTES

Pork fat
4 pounds fresh
   pork shoulder,
   boned and diced
2 green peppers
2 red peppers

4 cups frozen, peeled tomatoes or
   canned tomatoes
2 teaspoons Worchestershire sauce
2 teaspoons salt

Fry fat from pork shoulder in a large Dutch oven. Add boned pork and brown. Remove seeds from peppers and cut in large dice. Add with remaining ingredients to pork. Cover and simmer about 1 hour. Cool and ladle into two 6 to 8 cup freezer containers. Chill. Seal, label and date.

Storage time: 2 months.

To serve: Defrost one container and place in saucepan. Add 3 medium potatoes peeled and cut in large pieces and 3 white turnips peeled and diced. Cover and simmer 30 minutes or until potatoes and turnips are tender. If desired, gravy may be thickened with a little flour. Add salt and pepper, if needed. Makes 6 servings.

HAM PATTIES

4 cups left-over chopped ham
4 cups mashed potatoes

1 medium onion, grated
2 teaspoons prepared mustard

Mix ham lightly with remaining ingredients until well blended. Shape into patties about 2-1/2 inches across and 1 inch thick. Chill. Wrap, with 2 thicknesses of wax paper between each patty, in suitable serving size packages. Makes about 18 patties. Seal, label and date.

Storage time: 2 months.

To serve: Defrost ham patties. Mix 1 egg with 2 tablespoons water. Dip patties in egg and then in dry brown crumbs. Brown in butter, turning to brown both sides. Serve at once.

KABOBS

Alternate enough tender cubes of beef, lamb or veal with small onions and pieces of green pepper on each skewer for one serving. Wrap each individually in plastic wrap and freeze. When frozen store in plastic freezer bags. Seal, label and date.

Storage time: 2 to 3 months.

To serve: Remove number of kabobs needed and place in a flat glass dish. Mix 1/2 cup vegetable oil, 1/4 cup wine vinegar, 1/2 teaspoon each salt and garlic salt, 1/2 teaspoon each crushed rosemary and summer savory. Pour over meat. As meat defrosts, turn kabobs in marinade occasionally. (While meat is frozen marinade will cling to kabobs.) This amount of marinade is sufficient for 6 kabobs. When meat is completely defrosted, broil or grill 5 to 8 minutes, turning.

SANDWICH MEAT—MEAT LOAF

2 pounds ground beef	1 tablespoon grated onion, if desired
1/2 pound chopped bologna	2 eggs, slightly beaten
1 cup soft bread crumbs	1 teaspoon salt
1 cup chili sauce	Freshly ground pepper

Combine all ingredients and mix lightly until blended. Pack into a 9 x 5-inch loaf pan and bake in a 350° F. oven for 1-1/4 hours. While still warm, pour off accumulated fat in pan. Chill meat loaf. Cut into sandwich thick slices and wrap for freezing with a double thickness of wax paper between slices, in suitable serving size packages. Seal, label and date.

Storage time: 2 months.

To serve: Defrost and use for sandwiches or on a cold plate instead of cold cuts.

CASSEROLE PIMONDO

1 pound sliced beef liver,
    defrosted
Boiling water
2 tablespoons butter or
    margarine
2 tablespoons flour
1-1/2 cups beef stock

2 tablespoons chopped celery
1/2 cup sliced, stuffed olives
1 teaspoon salt
1 tablespoon Worcestershire sauce
2 hard cooked eggs
1/2 cup buttered bread crumbs

Cover liver with boiling water and simmer 5 minutes. Drain, cut into 1/2-inch cubes.

Melt butter, add flour, gradually pour in beef stock, stirring. Cook and stir until mixture is thickened. Add liver, celery, olives, seasonings and mashed egg yolks. Pour into a buttered 6-cup casserole. Top with bread crumbs and chopped egg whites. Bake at 350° F. 20 minutes or until bubbly. Makes 4 servings.

DEVILED BEEF CHUCK STEAK

2 pounds (about) beef chuck steak,
    defrosted
2 tablespoons flour
2 tablespoons butter or
    margarine
1 large onion, sliced

3 tablespoons vinegar
1/8 teaspoon paprika
1 teaspoon salt
Freshly ground pepper to taste
1 cup hot water
1 teaspoon prepared mustard

Sprinkle steak with flour and brown on both sides in butter. Place in a buttered flat casserole. Add onion slices. Mix remaining ingredients in skillet and scrape and stir to remove brown crust. Heat and pour over meat and onions. Cover and bake at 350° F. for one hour or until tender. Slice and serve with gravy. Makes 4 to 6 servings.

CURRIED LAMB WITH RICE

2 pounds lean lamb breast
    or shoulder, defrosted
2 tablespoons corn oil
1 bay leaf
2 small onions
6 whole black peppers

1 tablespoon chopped parsley
1 teaspoon salt
1/4 cup flour
1 to 2 teaspoons curry powder
1/2 teaspoon powdered ginger
2 tablespoons water

Cut lamb in cubes and brown in oil on all sides. When browned, cover with hot water, add bay leaf, onions, pepper, parsley and salt. Cover and simmer 1 to 1-1/2 hours or until meat is tender. Strain stock and measure 2 cups. Mix flour with curry powder, ginger and the 2 tablespoons of water to make a paste. With a whisk, stir into 2 cups of stock. Cook and stir over low heat until thickened. Add lamb. Reheat, if necessary. Serve over hot cooked rice. Makes 4 to 6 servings.

BAKED LAMB CHOPS

6 rib or shoulder lamb chops,
    defrosted
2 tablespoons corn oil
1 teaspoon salt
Fresh ground pepper to taste

1 frozen green pepper cut
    in rings or slices
1 large onion, sliced
1 lemon, sliced
2 cups frozen tomato juice,
    defrosted

Brown chops in hot oil and place in baking dish as browned. Sprinkle with salt and pepper. Top each chop with green pepper, an onion slice, a lemon slice and pour tomato juice over all. Cover and bake at 350° F. for 1-1/2 hours or until tender. Makes 6 servings.

DERRY BEEF ROAST

4 to 5 pound beef pot roast,
  defrosted
1 cup chopped onions
1 clove garlic, minced
1-1/2 teaspoons salt
2-1/2 cups boiling water

1 teaspoon sugar
1/8 teaspoon allspice
1 teaspoon Worcestershire sauce
1 tablespoon lemon juice
1/2 cup tomato juice
3/4 cup chopped celery

Brown beef on all sides in a kettle which can be tightly covered. Pour off any fat which has accumulated. Add remaining ingredients. Cover tightly and cook until fork tender, about 3 hours, over low heat. When done, remove meat to platter and keep hot. Measure liquid, add 1-1/2 tablespoons flour mixed to a paste with water for each cup of liquid. Return to pan and cook and stir until thickened. Slice meat and serve with gravy. Makes 6 servings with left-overs.

PORK CHOPS BRAISED WITH FRUIT

4 large frozen pork chops,
  defrosted
1/2 teaspoon salt

Freshly ground pepper
4 slices canned pineapple or
  peeled fresh orange slices

Trim fat from pork chops and fry out fat in skillet. Brown pork chops on both sides in pork fat. Sprinkle with salt and pepper. Place a slice of pineapple or orange on each chop. Cover and cook slowly 1 hour or more until pork chops are tender. If necessary a little water may be added to the skillet. Serve pork chops with fruit and pan juices. Makes 4 servings.

ROAST SHOULDER OF LAMB

4 to 5 pounds frozen shoulder
    of lamb, defrosted
2 teaspoons salt
Freshly ground pepper
4 cups soft, fresh bread crumbs
1/2 cup chopped onion

1/2 cup chopped celery
1 egg, beaten
1 teaspoon poultry seasoning
1 cup dry white wine
2 tablespoons flour

Remove bone from lamb shoulder and cut a pocket in the meat. Rub inside and outside of lamb with salt and pepper. Mix bread crumbs with onion, celery, egg and poultry seasoning. Stuff pocket and close with skewers or by sewing.

Place stuffed lamb on a rack in a roasting pan. Roast at 300° F. for 2 to 2-1/2 hours (about 35 minutes per pound). Baste with white wine during cooking. Remove to warm platter. Mix flour with 1/2 cup cold water. Measure pan juices and add water or bouillon to make 2 cups. Add flour mixture to pan juices. Cook and stir over low heat until gravy boils and is thickened. Season to taste. Serve with lamb. Serves 8 to 10.

BARBECUED PORK CHOPS

6 pork shoulder chops,
  defrosted
1 can (8-ounce) Spanish style
  tomato sauce
1/2 cup frozen diced onion
1/4 cup catsup
2 tablespoons vinegar

2 tablespoons brown sugar
1 tablespoon prepared mustard
1 tablespoon
  worcestershire sauce
1 teaspoon salt
1/8 teaspoon pepper

Brown pork chops on both sides. Combine remaining ingredients. Pour over chops and simmer, covered for 45 minutes or until chops are tender. Makes 6 servings.

SWEET–SOUR PORK

1-1/4 pounds lean pork shoulder,
  defrosted
2 tablespoons oil
1 teaspoon garlic salt
1/8 teaspoon
  freshly ground pepper
1-3/4 cups water

1-1/2 cups diced green pepper,
  defrosted
1/2 cup raisins
3 tablespoons cornstarch
1/3 cup sugar
1/4 cup soy sauce
1/3 cup vinegar
3 cups cooked rice

Cut pork into 1-inch cubes. Brown in hot oil. Add seasonings and water. Cover and simmer until meat is tender, about 40 minutes. Add green pepper and raisins and cook 10 minutes longer. Mix cornstarch, sugar, soy sauce and vinegar. Stir into meat mixture. Cook and stir until broth is clear and thickened. Serve over hot rice. Makes 6 servings.

BEEF STEW RHINELAND

2 pounds frozen beef chuck,
   defrosted
2 tablespoons bacon fat
2 cups cold water

3/4 cup red wine
3 large onions, sliced
1 teaspoon salt
4 whole cloves, crushed

Dumplings

1-1/2 cups all purpose flour
3 teaspoons baking powder
3/4 teaspoon salt

1 tablespoon shortening
3/4 cup milk

Cut beef into small cubes and brown quickly in bacon fat. Add water, wine, onions, salt and cloves and simmer, covered, 2 hours or until meat is tender.

To make dumplings:

Mix flour with baking powder and salt in a bowl. Cut in shortening and lightly mix in milk. Place by spoonsful on top of stew. Cover and simmer 10 minutes. Remove lid and simmer 10 minutes longer. Serve dumplings with stew. Makes 6 servings.

SOUR CREAM VEAL FRICASSEE

2 pounds boneless veal
   shoulder, defrosted
2 tablespoons flour
2 large onions, sliced
2 tablespoons butter or
   margarine

1 teaspoon salt
1/2 teaspoon paprika
Freshly ground pepper to taste
1 cup dairy sour cream

Cut veal into 1-inch cubes. Sprinkle with flour. Brown with onion in butter. Add salt, paprika and pepper. Cover and cook slowly about one hour or until tender. Add a small amount of water, if necessary. Just before serving stir in sour cream and heat. Makes 6 servings.

PORK CHOPS, HANSON

1 cup cranberries, defrosted
1/2 cup sugar
1/4 cup water

4 medium sweet potatoes, cooked
4 pork chops, defrosted
1 teaspoon salt

In a buttered, flat 6 cup casserole, place washed cranberries, sugar and water. Peel and slice sweet potatoes and place on cranberries. Arrange pork chops on top of sweet potatoes and sprinkle with salt. Cover and bake at 350° F. for 45 minutes. Uncover and bake 15 minutes longer, or until pork chops are browned and tender. Makes 4 servings.

POULTRY

The classification poultry includes chickens, fowl, capon, turkeys, ducks, geese and such specialties as Cornish game hens. Poultry to be frozen should be chosen with care, properly packaged and frozen and stored at 0° F.

How to's With Uncooked Poultry

- Consider the greatest use for poultry in choosing how to buy and freeze it. If you prefer broiled chicken to fried you might freeze chicken in halves or quarters instead of cut up.
- Poultry as purchased in the market, unless especially arranged for, is not packaged for freezing. Remove the giblet-neck package, clean and properly freezer wrap before freezing.
- Do not stuff poultry before freezing. It takes longer for the cold to penetrate to freeze the product and the reverse in defrosting, thus giving more opportunity for spoilage.
- In preparing broilers for freezer, choose 2-1/2 to 3-pound broiler-fryers. Remove wing tips, cut on either side of the backbone to remove it, cut chicken through breast and leave in halves or cut into quarters depending on taste. Wrap pieces individually for easy separation when defrosting. Freeze and store in plastic freezer bags or overwrap the number of pieces needed for serving at one time in one package. Label, date and freeze.
- Backbones, necks, giblets, wing tips and bony pieces can all go into a bag labeled "chicken pieces for soup" before freezing, or make chicken broth at once and freeze that.
- When purchasing commercially frozen poultry for the home freezer, mark it with date purchased so oldest purchases will be used first. Whole frozen turkeys and chickens have an optimum storage life of one year — so if those purchases are not clearly coded at the packing plant as to date frozen or date to be used, plan on home storage of no more than 8 to 10 months for the best tasting bird. Ducks and geese have an optimum storage period of 6 months, so dating their purchases is especially important.
- When fresh turkey is a good buy, consider having it cut into pieces by the butcher and freezing some in that form for future use. Breast sections can be roasted, dark meat braised for many tasty dishes. Wings and bony pieces can be used for soup.
- When freezing whole birds, clean well inside and out and drain. Compact the bird by tying wings and legs close to the body. Conform freezer wrapping close to body to exclude air. Seal, label and date.
- Disjoint chicken for frying. Wash and dry. Wrap pieces individually, freeze and store enough pieces for a family serving in a freezer bag. Seal, label and date. The extra effort in wrapping pieces singly at freezing time is worth it. The chicken pieces defrost quickly for last minute menu planning.

When you have the opportunity to freeze home raised poultry, here are some guidelines.

Select birds of the size and weight best suited to your needs. Chickens may be frozen for broiling or frying at 8 to 10 weeks of age and for roasting at 3 to 5 months. Older chickens may be frozen for stewing. Turkeys may be frozen for roasting at 6 to 7 months and ducks at 6 to 8 weeks.

Prepare killed bird by removing feathers, pinfeathers and singe off any hair, if necessary. Cut off head, feet, remove oil sac at top of tail. Cut a circle around vent below tail and a crosswise slit at base of breast to remove internal organs. Slit skin lengthwise at back of neck, slip skin down and remove crop and windpipe. Cut neck short and reserve. Wash well under running water. Chill bird from 12 to 24 hours in the refrigerator before freezing. The bird should be no longer stiff and the wings should rotate easily. The birds may either be frozen whole or cut up as desired.

Fresh Poultry to Freeze and Storage Time

	in freezer at 0° F.
Chicken and Turkey (whole)	12 months
Chicken pieces	9 months
Turkey pieces	6 months
Ducks and Geese (whole)	6 months
Giblets	3 months
Chicken livers	3 months

Freezing Cooked Poultry

Cooked poultry for freezing can be especially prepared for that purpose, or it can be leftover poultry. Any kind of poultry can be cooked and frozen satisfactorily.

How to's With Cooked Poultry

- Cooked poultry that is frozen without gravy or broth has a shorter freezer life. This includes fried chicken, roasted poultry that is frozen as slices or in sandwiches.
- Remove cooked poultry from carcass. Freeze carcass separately to use for soup later.
- When roasting poultry especially to freeze, do not stuff. This means that the bird may be cooled more quickly and the cooked meat gotten into the freezer faster. As with all frozen products, the fresher it goes into the freezer the better the result.
- Divide cooked meat into large and small pieces. Package separately in meal size amounts. If packed without gravy or broth, wrap in freezer wrap and seal, label and date. If packed in broth or gravy, pack in rigid containers leaving headspace for expansion.
- To freeze fried chicken, use your favorite recipe. Chill the finished pieces. Either wrap individually and freeze in family size portions in a freezer bag, or tray freeze and store at once in a freezer bag or vapor-proof freezer box. Seal, label and date either pack.

Cooked Poultry to Freeze and Storage Time

	in freezer at 0° F.
Pieces (covered with broth)	6 months
Pieces (not covered with broth)	1 month
Cooked Poultry Dishes	6 months
Fried Chicken	4 months

Defrosting Whole Birds

The best method to defrost whole frozen birds (and all poultry for that matter) is in the refrigerator. Remove freezer wrappings, place bird on tray, cover loosely with wax paper or pliable wrap and put in refrigerator. Timetable for thawing whole birds in refrigerator:

Chickens	
4 pounds and over	1 to 1-1/2 days
Less than 4 pounds	12 to 16 hours
Ducks, 3 to 5 pounds	1 to 1-1/2 days
Geese, 4 to 14 pounds	1 to 2 days
Turkeys	
18 pounds and over	2 to 3 days
Less than 18 pounds	1 to 2 days

If you get caught short of defrosting time, birds in waterproof packaging can be all or partially defrosted in cold water to speed up defrosting. Change water often.

Directions for Roast Turkey

Defrost turkey in refrigerator.

Season inside of turkey with salt; or fill cavity with stuffing.

Fasten neck skin to back and tie legs together. Turn wing tips under back.

Place turkey, breast side up, on rack in a shallow pan. If a thermometer is used, place it in center of thigh meat next to body. Do not let thermometer touch bone.

Loosen legs when turkey is partly cooked.

Roast at 325° F. until leg moves up and down easily, or until the thigh temperature reaches 180° to 185° F., and the stuffing in the body cavity reaches at least 165° F. (Insert thermometer in stuffing after removing from thigh).

Approximate roasting times at 325° F. for stuffed turkeys:

6 to 8 pounds	3 to 3-1/2 hours
8 to 12 pounds	3-1/2 to 4-1/2 hours
12 to 16 pounds	4-1/2 to 5-1/2 hours
16 to 20 pounds	5-1/2 to 6-1/2 hours
20 to 24 pounds	6-1/2 to 7 hours

During roasting, baste turkeys with pan drippings or melted butter. Cover with aluminum foil if skin is browning too fast.

Bread Stuffing for Turkey

1-1/2 cups butter or	2 teaspoons salt
or margarine	1/4 teaspoon freshly
3/4 cup finely chopped onion	ground pepper
1 cup finely chopped celery	1 teaspoon poultry seasoning
3 to 4 quarts stale	1/2 teaspoon ground sage
bread cubes	1/2 teaspoon thyme

Heat butter in a large skillet or saucepan. Add onion and celery and cook slowly until tender but not browned. Add bread cubes and seasoning and stir until bread is lightly browned. Cool. This makes enough stuffing for a 12 to 16 pound turkey.

Variations:

Oyster: Add 2 cups oysters, drained and chopped. Cook oysters with celery and onion.

Sausage: Crumble 1 pound sausage meat and brown lightly. Remove sausage from pan and substitute fat for half the butter.

ROAST DUCK A L' ORANGE

1 frozen duck (5 pounds)
   defrosted
1 teaspoon salt
1/8 teaspoon
   freshly ground pepper
1 small onion, sliced
1 large carrot, diced
1 stalk celery, diced
3 cups boiling water
1/2 cup orange juice

2 teaspoons lemon juice
2 tablespoons currant jelly
2 tablespoons
   slivered orange peel
1 tablespoon
   slivered lemon peel
1 tablespoon cornstarch
2 tablespoons cold water
1 orange, sliced

Wash and dry duck. Sprinkle with salt and pepper. Put vegetables in open roaster and add boiling water. Place duck on vegetables and roast at 350° F. for 1-1/2 to 2 hours (20-25 minutes per pound) or until duck is tender, basting with pan juices during roasting.

Transfer duck to a warm platter and keep warm.

Strain pan juices into a saucepan. Add orange and lemon juice, currant jelly and peels. Cover and simmer 5 minutes. Mix cornstarch with water and add to mixture. Cook until clear and thickened. Serve with duck. Garnish duck on platter with orange slices. Makes 4 servings.

VERMONT CHICKEN

2 broiler-fryer chickens cut into pieces	Freshly ground pepper to taste 1/2 cup vegetable oil
1/4 cup flour	1 cup frozen applesauce,
1/2 teaspoon poultry seasoning	defrosted
1 teaspoon salt	3 tablespoons maple syrup

Cut chicken into serving size pieces. (Save bony pieces for broth.) Mix flour with poultry seasoning, salt and pepper. Sprinkle over chicken pieces. Heat vegetable oil in skillet and brown chicken on all sides. As pieces brown, transfer to two flat aluminum freezer dishes. When all chicken is browned, mix apple sauce with maple syrup and spread 1/2 cup over each pan of chicken. Cover and chill. Then label, date and freeze.

Storage time: 4 to 6 months.

To serve: Remove lid from chicken in one pan. Place in a 375° F. oven and cover loosely with foil. Bake about 40 minutes (if chicken was not defrosted) and 20 to 25 minutes for defrosted chicken. Remove foil and spinkle with 1/2 cup grated Cheddar cheese. Bake 5 minutes longer. Makes 4 servings.

CHICKEN CASSEROLE

2 broiler-fryer chickens, cut up
8 cups water
2-1/2 teaspoons salt
1 teaspoon garlic powder
1/4 cup butter or margarine
4 cups diced celery
2 cups diced onion
1 pound small macaroni,
   cooked and drained
1/4 cup cornstarch
1 jar (2 ounces) pimiento,
   drained and chopped

Combine chicken with water, salt and garlic powder, and cook until tender, 30 to 40 minutes. Cool chicken in broth. Remove chicken from bones. Reserve broth and chicken. If desired, this step may be done a day in advance. Refrigerate chicken and broth.

Heat butter in a large saucepan and saute celery and onion until tender but not browned. Add 1 quart chicken broth. Mix cornstarch with 1/2 cup cooled broth and stir into broth in saucepan. Cook and stir until mixture boils and is thickened and clear. Taste and add additional salt and pepper, if needed. Gently mix in chicken pieces, macaroni and pimiento. Spoon into two foil-lined, 2-quart casseroles allowing enough foil up over edges to cover casserole. Chill, cover top and seal, label, date and freeze. When food is frozen, it may be removed from casserole.

Overwrap with plastic wrap.

Storage time: 3 to 4 months.

To serve: Unwrap casserole and place in original casserole dish in which it was frozen well buttered. Cover lightly and bake in a 375° F. oven 50-60 minutes. Uncover, sprinkle with 1/2 cup buttered bread crumbs and bake until lightly browned. Makes 4 servings.

If casserole is defrosted before baking, reduce baking time to 40 minutes.

CHICKEN LUNCHEON SALAD

4 cups tomato vegetable juice	1 cup finely diced celery
4 tablespoons unflavored gelatin	1 tablespoon chopped parsley
1-1/2 cups diced, cooked chicken	1-1/3 cups mayonnaise
1 cup cooked green beans, cut in pieces	1 cup cream, whipped
	1/4 cup cold water
1 cup cold cooked rice	1/4 cup chopped green pepper
1 teaspoon salt	

Combine 1 cup tomato juice with 2 tablespoons gelatin. When gelatin is softened, stir over heat until dissolved. Mix with remaining tomato juice and chill. Then freeze until mushy, stirring occasionally.

Meanwhile, combine chicken, beans, rice, green pepper, celery and parsley. Mix mayonnaise and whipped cream. Soften remaining gelatin in cold water and dissolve over heat. Add salt. Gently stir into mayonnaise mixture and then combine with chicken mixture. Spread half of the frozen tomato mixture in two 8x8x2-inch aluminum foil pans. Divide the chicken salad between the two pans, spooning carefully onto the frozen tomato juice. Top with remaining tomato juice and freeze at once. Cover, label and date.

Storage time: 6 months.

To serve: Cut into squares and serve frozen on lettuce leaves. Whole recipe makes 16 to 20 servings.

CHICKEN BREASTS, DE LUXE

8 whole chicken breasts, boned	1 teaspoon grated orange peel
1 teaspoon salt	1/4 cup finely chopped
Freshly ground pepper to taste	green onion
2 cups stuffing mix	1/4 cup ground almonds
1/2 teaspoon powdered thyme	1/3 cup orange juice

Lay boned chicken breasts skin side down on board. Mix remaining ingredients. Divide evenly between chicken breasts. Fold edges of chicken over stuffing and secure with toothpicks. Wrap individually in freezer wrap. Seal and freeze. Put in freezer bag and label, date and return to freezer.

Storage time: 4 to 6 months.

To serve: Defrost 4 breasts and dip in flour. Brown in 4 to 6 tablespoons butter or margarine. Place in baking dish. Pour 1/2 to 3/4 cup orange juice over chicken. Baked covered, 30 minutes at 375° F. Uncover and bake 15 minutes longer. Sprinkle with 1/4 cup chopped parsley. Remove toothpicks before serving. Makes 4 servings.

Recipes to use food from freezer

CHICKEN MUSHROOM SKILLET

2 tablespoons butter	1/4 cup chicken broth
or margarine	1/4 cup dry sherry wine
1 cup sliced frozen mushrooms,	1/2 teaspoon dried Rosemary
defrosted	Salt and pepper to taste
1/4 cup chopped parsley	Fried Chicken pieces for 4 servings

Heat butter in skillet. Add mushrooms and saute 2 to 3 minutes. Add parsley, broth, sherry and seasonings. Bring to a boil. Add chicken pieces and cook over low heat, covered, about 20 to 30 minutes. If necessary add a little additional sherry to skillet during cooking. Serve chicken with sauce. Makes 4 servings.

CHICKEN TAMALE PIE

1 cup corn meal
1 cup cold water
1-1/2 teaspoons salt
4 cups boiling water
6 cups diced, cooked chicken
1 can (16-ounce) tomato sauce
   with mushrooms

5 cups whole kernel corn,
   defrosted
1/4 cup sugar
1/4 cup vegetable oil
1/2 cup sliced, stuffed olives
1/4 teaspoon cayenne pepper
1/4 teaspoon
   freshly ground pepper

Combine cornmeal with cold water and salt in a large saucepan. Add boiling water and cook and stir until mixture boils. Cover and cook over low heat 15 minutes, stirring occasionally. Cool to room temperature.

Grease 2 2-quart baking dishes and line with aluminum foil, leaving enough to cover top of dish. Spread each dish with cornmeal mush on bottom and sides. Combine remaining ingredients and spoon into cornmeal lined casseroles. Cover top with foil and chill. Then seal, label, date and freeze. Remove from casseroles and overwrap with plastic freezer wrap. Return to freezer.

Storage time: 4 to 6 months. Makes 2 casseroles.

To serve: Remove wrappings and place in greased casserole in which dish was frozen. Defrost overnight in refrigerator. Sprinkle 1 cup grated Parmesan cheese over top and bake at 350° F. for 45 minutes to 1 hour or until hot and bubbly. Makes 6 servings.

DIXIE CHICKEN CASSEROLE

1 cup regular rice
1 can (4-ounce) pimientos
2 tablespoons chopped parsley
1-1/2 cups cooked, diced chicken
1/2 cup chopped almonds

1 cup sliced fresh mushrooms,
    sauted
2 cups chicken broth
2 tablespoons flour
Salt and pepper to taste

Grease and line a 2-quart casserole with foil, leaving enough to bring over the top.

Cook rice in boiling salted water until tender, 12 to 15 minutes. Drain, mix with pimientos, which have been drained and chopped, and parsley. Place one-third of the rice in casserole. Mix chicken with sauted mushrooms and almonds and put one-half over rice. Add a layer of rice, a layer of chicken and a layer of rice. Mix chicken broth with flour, season to taste with salt and pepper and pour over casserole. Freeze. When frozen cover with aluminum foil. Seal, label and date. Remove from casserole and overwrap with plastic freezer wrap. Return to freezer.

Storage time: Up to 3 months.

To use: Remove wrappings and place in original casserole in which frozen. Dot top with butter. Defrost. Bake at 350° F. for 1 hour. Makes 6 to 8 servings.

CREAMED CHICKEN RACINE

1 tablespoon butter or
    margarine
1/2 cup chopped celery
1-1/2 cups frozen green beans,
    defrosted
2 cups diced cooked chicken

1 can (10½-ounce)
    cream of mushroom soup
1/2 soup can milk
1/2 teaspoon oregano
Freshly ground pepper to taste
Hot cooked rice

Heat butter in a large saucepan, add celery and cook over low heat until tender. Cut green beans into 1/4-inch pieces. Add to celery and cook covered, stirring occasionally, about 10 minutes or until beans are tender. Add chicken, soup, milk, oregano and pepper. Mix lightly and continue cooking over low heat, 10 minutes, stirring. Serve over hot cooked rice. Makes 6 servings.

Recipes to use food from freezer

CHICKEN TOMAS

2 whole chicken breasts,
    defrosted
1 cup frozen peas
1/2 package dry onion soup mix

1 cup dairy sour cream
1/2 cup dry white wine
Salt and pepper to taste
1/2 teaspoon paprika

Bone and cut chicken breasts into large pieces. Arrange with peas in a buttered 4 cup casserole. Mix remaining ingredients. Pour over chicken. Bake at 350° F. 40 minutes or until chicken is tender. Makes 4 servings.

Recipes to use food from the freezer

CHICKEN DOMINIC

2 slices bacon
Cut up chicken to serve 4,
    defrosted
1 clove garlic, crushed
1 medium onion, sliced
4 frozen mushrooms, sliced

1/2 cup dry white wine
1 cup frozen, chopped tomatoes
    (or 1 cup canned tomatoes)
1 tablespoon chopped parsley
1 teaspoon salt
Freshly ground pepper to taste

Cut bacon in 1-inch pieces and fry until crisp. Push to one side and brown chicken pieces with garlic, onion and mushrooms in bacon fat. Add remaining ingredients and cover and simmer about 30 minutes or until chicken is tender. Serve chicken with sauce. Makes 4 servings.

FISH

Whether you have your own catch or fish purchased at the fish market in season, the freezer is a real boon for the preservation of fish. Fresh-frozen fish can add a delightful variety to the family menu. It should be processed quickly, stored at 0° F. in the freezer.

How to's With Fish

- Fish can be frozen: whole, as it comes from the water; drawn, whole fish with the entrails removed; dressed or pan dressed, whole fish with scales and entrails removed, usually with head, tail and fins removed; steaks, cross section slices about 3/4-inch thick from large dressed fish; fillets, sides of the fish, cut away lengthwise from the bone.
- Fish should be frozen as fresh as possible and handled carefully. It spoils and changes flavor quickly, so be certain to have the time to devote to the freezing preparations when fish are available.
- It is space saving to freeze fish in package form. Fish which has had all the waste parts removed takes up considerably less space in the freezer than whole fish. Separate fillets with double thicknesses of paper before overwrapping.
- Whole fish can be frozen in ice if desired. If the fish will fit a half gallon waxed milk carton, suspend whole or drawn fish in center of carton, surround with finely chopped ice, fill with water and freeze. Cover carton and label and date and return to freezer.
- Whole fish can also be ice glazed. Freeze fish. Remove from freezer and dip in cold water and let ice film freeze. Dip and freeze several times returning to freezer between dippings. To keep glaze intact, wrap fish in freezer wrap. Seal, label and date.
- Dip fillets and steaks of lean fish (flounder, ocean perch, haddock, pickerel, scup, bass) in a brine solution prepared by dissolving 2/3 cup salt in 1 gallon water. This reduces drip after thawing. Fatty fish (salmon, mackerel, tuna, trout, lake trout, striped bass) should not be brined.

Storage Chart for Fish

Fatty fish (salmon, mackerel, tuna, trout, lake trout, striped bass)

3 months

Lean fish (flounder, ocean perch, haddock, pickerel, scup, bass)

6 months

Cooking frozen fish

Because fish should be delicately cooked, it is best to always defrost it before cooking. Defrosting should be done in the refrigerator, or may be hastened by holding the packaged fish under cold, running water.

SHELLFISH

Lobster, crab, shrimp, oysters, scallops and clams can all be frozen for future use. As with fish, only the freshest products should be frozen, and stored at 0° F.

How to's With Shellfish
CRABS AND LOBSTERS
- Boil live lobsters and crabs in a solution of 1/2 cup salt to 1 gallon of water for 10 to 15 minutes. Cool rapidly in ice water and pick meat from shells. Pack in freezer containers in family size portions. Seal, label and date.

SHRIMP
- Shrimp may be frozen cooked or raw.
- To freeze raw shrimp, wash, remove heads and sand vein. Wash in brine, (1 teaspoon salt per quart water) drain and package in freezer containers in family size portions. Seal, label and date.
- To freeze cooked shrimp, wash in brine (as above) and cook in a solution of 1/2 cup salt to 1 gallon water for 10 minutes. Chill immediately in ice water. Shell and remove vein. Rinse and package in freezer containers in family size portions. Seal, label and date.
- Both shrimps (cooked and raw) can be tray frozen if desired. Package shrimp in plastic bags or freezer containers immediately after it becomes frozen. Seal, label and date and return to freezer.

OYSTERS
- Shuck oysters and reserve liquid. Wash in brine of 1/3 cup salt to 1 gallon water. Drain. Package with reserved liquid in freezer containers in family size portions. Seal, label and date.

SCALLOPS
- Shuck scallops and discard liquid. Wash in a brine of 1/3 cup salt to 1 gallon water. Drain. Package in freezer containers in family size portions. Seal, label, and date.

CLAMS (Cherrystone and Littleneck & similar clams eaten raw)
- Shuck clams and reserve liquid. Wash in a brine of 1/3 cup salt to 1 gallon water. Drain. Package with reserved liquid in freezer containers in family size portions. Seal, label and date.

CLAMS (Quahogs and Steamers)
- Steam clams open to make meat removal easier. Freeze clams with or without juice, whole or chopped, in freezer containers in family size portions. Use for clam chowder or cooked clam dishes.

Storage Chart for Shellfish

Crab and Lobster .... 3 months
Shrimp .... 6 months
Oysters, Scallops, Clams .... 4 months

Using frozen shellfish

As with fish, shellfish should be defrosted before use. This is best done in the refrigerator.

Recipes for freezing

Fish recipes as a rule, do not lend themselves too well to freezing because fish toughens from too much cooking and long freezer storage. However, there are some thrifty ways to use the freezer for fish that are worth taking advantage of.

FISH STOCK

If you are cleaning whole fish to freeze, do not discard the heads and backbones. Wash them well and put them in a saucepot. Cover with water, add salt to taste, peppercorns, a few slices of onion and a small bay leaf. Bring to a boil, skim, and simmer 5 to 10 minutes. Cool rapidly (immerse pan in ice water) and strain liquid. Carefully remove all fish from bones and freeze with stock in freezer containers, leaving head space for expansion. Seal, label and date.

Storage time: about 3 months

To use: Each pint of this fish stock and fish can be used to make a good fish chowder or fish soup.

Recipes to use food from the freezer

FISH CHOWDER

2 slices bacon, diced	1/2 cup water
1 small onion, chopped	1 pint fish and stock, defrosted
2 medium potatoes,	1 cup nonfat dry milk
peeled and diced	Salt and pepper to taste

In a medium saucepan, fry bacon and onion together until bacon is crisp and onion tender. Add potatoes and water and cook, covered, 10 to 15 minutes or until potatoes are tender. Pour off enough fish stock to mix with and dissolve dry milk and add it with remaining fish stock and fish to potatoes. Heat, but do not boil. Add salt and pepper to taste. Makes about 4 cups.

FISH SOUP

2 tablespoons butter or margarine	1/4 teaspoon leaf thyme
1 medium onion, sliced	1/4 teaspoon leaf oregano
1 carrot, peeled and sliced	1 pint fish and stock, defrosted
1 tomato, peeled and diced	Salt and pepper to taste

Heat butter or margarine in medium saucepan. Fry onion until golden. Add carrots, tomato, thyme, oregano and fish stock. Cook, covered, 10 to 15 minutes or until carrots are tender. Add fish and heat, but do not boil. Add salt and pepper to taste. Makes about 4 cups.

Recipes for freezing

FISH FLAKES

If there are many small pieces of fish left from cleaning which are impractical to freeze, wash and poach (cook below the boiling point) in the smallest amount of water possible. When fish flakes, 4 to 5 minutes, cool rapidly and freeze in containers in family size portions. Seal, label and date.

Storage time: about 3 months.

To use: Use fish flakes for these easy fish cakes, fish salad or scalloped fish recipes.

Fish Cakes: Mix well equal parts of defrosted fish flakes and mashed potatoes. Season with salt and pepper. Dip in cornmeal and fry over medium heat in bacon fat. 1 pint of fish and 1 pint of potatoes makes about 8 cakes.

Fish Salad: Mix defrosted fish flakes with finely chopped celery, salt, pepper and lemon juice to taste. Moisten with mayonnaise. Serve as a salad or a sandwich filling.

Scalloped Fish: Mix about 2 cups of defrosted fish flakes with 1 can condensed cream of mushroom soup mixed with 1/2 cup milk. Layer in a 1 quart casserole with two boiled potatoes thinly sliced. Sprinkle top with grated American cheese. Bake at 375° F. for 20 minutes or until bubbly. Makes 4 servings.

To Fry Fish: Defrost and dip fillets or steaks in beaten egg and then in flour. Fry in shallow fat over moderately high heat, turning to brown both sides. Thin fillets should cook no longer than 3 to 4 minutes, steaks 3/4 inch thick 5 to 6 minutes.

To Broil Fish: Defrost and place fillets or steaks on greased broiler rack. Spread with softened butter, sprinkle with lemon juice and a layer of fine, dry bread crumbs. Sprinkle with paprika. Broil 3 inches from source of heat 3 to 5 minutes depending on thickness. Fish steaks less than 1 inch thick do not need to be turned.

Recipes to use food from the freezer

FISH FILLETS WITH CURRIED SHRIMP SAUCE

1-1/2 pounds fish fillets, defrosted	1 can (10 ounce) frozen cream of shrimp soup, defrosted
Seasoned salt	1 to 2 teaspoons curry powder
3/4 cup dry white wine	1/4 cup chopped parsley

Sprinkle fillets with seasoned salt. Roll each and fasten with toothpicks. Arrange rolled fillets in a flat buttered casserole. Mix soup with wine and curry powder and pour over fillets. Sprinkle with parsley. Bake at 350° F. 20 to 25 minutes or until fish flakes. Makes 4 servings.

Recipes to use food from the freezer

BAKED WHOLE FISH

3 to 4 pound whole fish, dressed, with head and tail on, defrosted	2 bay leaves
	1 teaspoon salt
	Freshly ground pepper to taste
1 medium onion, sliced	1 cup dairy sour cream
3 lemon slices	1/2 cup buttered crumbs

Place fish on foil strip in baking pan. Insert onion, lemon and bay leaf in cavity. Sprinkle fish with salt and pepper. Spread sour cream over fish. Bake at 375° F. for 40 minutes or until fish flakes easily. Ten minutes before fish is done sprinkle with bread crumbs. Use foil strip to transfer fish to platter. Garnish with additional lemon slices and parsley. Makes 4 to 6 servings.

FRIED SHRIMP

1-1/2 cups all purpose flour   3/4 cup evaporated milk
1/4 teaspoon salt   or light cream
1-1/2 teaspoons baking powder   Raw, peeled shrimp, defrosted
1 egg   Oil or fat for frying

Mix flour, salt and baking powder in a bowl. Beat egg and milk together and stir into flour mixture.

Heat oil or fat at least 2 inches deep to 360° F. (An electric skillet works well.) Dip shrimp in batter. Fry in hot fat, turning to brown both sides. Drain on absorbent paper. Serve hot with lemon slices or soy sauce. Makes enough batter for 18 large or more small shrimp.

RICE OYSTER SCALLOP

2 cups hot cooked rice   1/2 teaspoon salt
Softened butter or margarine   1 cup milk
2 tablespoons butter or   1/4 cup cubed sharp cheese
    margarine   1 pint oysters, defrosted
2 tablespoons flour   1/2 cup buttered crumbs
1 tablespoon prepared mustard

Spread rice on bottom and sides of a well buttered flat casserole or a 9 or 10 inch pie plate. Melt 2 tablespoons butter in saucepan. Add flour, mustard and salt and mix well. Stir in milk and cook and stir until mixture boils and is thickened. Add cheese and stir until melted. Add oysters. Spoon into center of rice. Sprinkle with bread crumbs. Bake at 375° F. 15 minutes or until bubbly. Makes 4 servings.

MARINATED BROILED SCALLOPS

1/3 cup soy sauce
1/3 cup lemon juice
1/3 cup salad oil

1/2 teaspoon seasoned pepper
1-1/2 pints scallops,
    defrosted

Combine soy sauce with lemon juice, salad oil and seasoned pepper. Combine with scallops and marinate in the refrigerator for several hours. Drain scallops and place on a greased shallow pan. Broil 3 inches from source of heat 2 to 3 minutes. Serves 6 people.

CLAM OMELET

4 tablespoons butter or
    margarine
6 eggs, slightly beaten
1 cup clams and juice, defrosted

1/2 teaspoon salt
Freshly ground pepper to taste
2 tablespoons chopped parsley

Heat butter in a 7 or 8 inch skillet. Mix eggs with remaining ingredients, pour into hot butter. Cook slowly, pulling edges into center as the eggs cook. When eggs are done to suit taste fold and slide onto a platter. Makes 4 servings.

SCALLOPED CODFISH AND OYSTERS

2 tablespoons melted butter
or margarine
2 tablespoons lemon juice
1 tablespoon grated onion
Dash Tabasco
2 dozen frozen oysters,
defrosted

2 cups flaked, cooked,
fresh cod
1/4 cup oyster liquor
or white wine
1/2 teaspoon salt
1/2 cup buttered bread crumbs

Mix butter, lemon juice, onion and Tabasco. Dip oysters in the butter mixture.

Arrange half of fish flakes in a buttered 6 cup casserole. Place oysters on fish and top with remaining fish flakes. Pour oyster liquor or wine over fish and sprinkle with salt. Cover with buttered bread crumbs and bake at 450° F. for 20 minutes or until bubbly. Serve with Tartar Sauce.

BROILED FISH STEAKS

6 frozen fish steaks
(about 2 pounds), defrosted
2 tablespoons melted
butter or margarine

2 tablespoons lemon juice
1 teaspoon salt
1/2 teaspoon paprika
Freshly ground pepper to taste

Place fish steaks in a greased, flat, flame proof baking pan. Spread with butter, lemon juice and sprinkle with salt, paprika and pepper. Broil 4-inches from source of heat 10 to 15 minutes, or until fish flakes easily with a fork. Baste once during broiling with liquid in pan. Makes 6 servings.

GRILLED FISH IN FOIL

Aluminum foil (heavy duty)
2 pounds frozen fish fillets,
   defrosted
2 green peppers
2 medium onions

1/4 cup melted butter
   or margarine
2 tablespoons lemon juice
1 teaspoon salt
1 teaspoon paprika
Freshly ground pepper to taste

Cut aluminum foil into 6 12-inch squares and butter well. Cut fish into 6 portions and place each portion on a square of foil. Clean and slice peppers and peel and slice onions and arrange on fish. Brush with melted butter and lemon juice and sprinkle with salt, paprika and pepper. Bring foil up over food and close edges with tight double fold. Place on a grill about 5-inches from moderately hot coals. Bake 45 to 60 minutes. Fish should flake easily with a fork. Makes 6 servings.

GAME AND GAME BIRDS

The quality of frozen game depends a great deal on the treatment of the game by the hunters. Here are some pointers to help assure a good quality of frozen product. Store frozen game at 0° F.

- All game should be gutted immediately after killing and cooled as soon as possible.
- Cleanliness is extremely important, since the shot may have punctured the intestines or caused shot damage to the muscles. Spoilage takes place rapidly under these conditions.
- Deer, bear and other large game can be handled for freezing like any other meat with a few exceptions: remove all visible fat before freezing because game fat becomes rancid quickly; remove as many bones as is practical. Many feel that an unpleasantly strong wild flavor results from bone marrow.
- Trim and discard bloodshot meat before freezing.
- Freeze game in family size portions.
- It is important to mark the cut so the game can be properly cooked.
- Hang game before freezing.
- Small game such as rabbits, squirrels and other small animals are dressed, cooled and then skinned. Refrigerate 24-36 hours until meat is no longer rigid, then wrap and freeze.
- If desired, small game may be cut into serving size pieces before freezing.
- Game birds including pheasant, geese, quail, ducks, etc., should be drawn as soon as possible after shooting. Cool promptly. Do not stack birds as this slows down cooling.
- Dress birds and refrigerate at least 24 hours before freezing.
- If several small birds are to be frozen together, wrap individually before overwrapping with freezer paper so they will separate easily for defrosting.
- For game birds, follow freezing procedures given for chicken.
- Remove all excess fat on geese before freezing as it becomes rancid quickly.

Observe state game laws for tagging and length of time in storage for game.

Recipes to use food from the freezer

VENISON STEAKS OR CHOPS

If the venison is young enough it can be broiled. Defrost the steaks or chops completely. Spread with butter and Worcestershire sauce. (When meat is turned, spread reverse side.) For a steak or chop 1-1/2 inches thick, broil 5 minutes on each side about 3 inches away from source of heat. Serve with pan juices and currant jelly.

RABBIT IN A PACKAGE

4 backs of rabbit, defrosted
1/4 pound salt pork, diced,
   rind removed
1/2 cup soft bread crumbs
1 cup tomato juice
1 garlic clove, minced

1/2 teaspoon nutmeg
Dash Tabasco sauce
1/2 teaspoon salt
Minced parsley,
      fresh tarragon, fresh sage

Wash backs, dry and place on pieces of aluminum foil large enough to form a package when folded around rabbit. Blend salt pork, crumbs, tomato juice, garlic, nutmeg, Tabasco and salt in a blender and spread over rabbit. Fasten foil around rabbit tightly enough to hold in steam and place in a roasting pan. Bake at 350° F. until tender, about 1 hour. To serve, open foil package on plate. Pass with dishes of minced herbs. Makes 4 servings.

ROAST LEG OF ANTELOPE

1 leg of antelope
   (leg and pelvic bone removed),
   about 5 pounds, defrosted
1/2 teaspoon salt
1/2 teaspoon garlic salt
2 teaspoons powdered oregano
1 medium onion, finely chopped

1/2 cup vegetable oil
2 cups water
1-1/2 cups dry red wine
1 cup tomato juice
1 bay leaf
2 tablespoons lemon juice

Soak antelope overnight in cold water. Dry well. Mix together salt, garlic salt, oregano and onion. Spread on meat and brown in hot oil in roasting pan. Bake at 350° F. 45 minutes to 1 hour. Add remaining ingredients and bake covered 2 hours longer. Let stand 10 minutes before slicing thinly to serve. Serve with pan juices. Makes 6 to 8 servings.

TEAL DUCKS, ROASTED

1/2 cup butter
1 teaspoon thick steak sauce
1/2 teaspoon salt
Freshly ground pepper

6 teal ducks, defrosted
6 slices bacon
6 slices white bread, toasted

Melt 1/4 cup butter and mix with steak sauce. Salt and pepper ducks and put a piece of remaining butter inside each. Wrap a slice of bacon around each duck and brush with melted butter mixture. Bake at 425° F. for 50 to 60 minutes or until tender. Baste often with pan juices. Serve on toast with pan juices. Makes 6 servings.

PHEASANTS

Pheasant for four servings
1/4 cup butter
Salt
Pepper

3 cups apples, chopped
2 teaspoons brown sugar
1/2 teaspoon cinnamon

Cut pheasants in halves or disjoint. Brown in butter and season with salt and pepper. Add chopped apples with brown sugar and cinnamon and brown. Spread in bottom of flat casserole. Arrange pheasant on apples. Cover with buttered parchment and cover with lid. Bake at 350° F. for 50 to 60 minutes. Serve with apples. Makes 4 servings.

BRAISED GROUSE

Grouse
Bacon
1 stalk celery
2 onions, sliced
Whole cloves

1 tablespoon butter
1 cup beef broth
1 tablespoon bourbon whiskey
1/4 cup white wine
Flour

Split grouse down back and spread open. Lay strips of bacon in pan, cut celery in pieces and sprinkle over bacon and several thick slices of onion with 2 or 3 cloves stuck in each. Lay birds skin side down on bacon and onion. Saute a medium sliced onion until golden in butter. Mix with beef broth and bourbon whiskey. Pour over the birds and cover with buttered parchment paper. Cover pan with lid and simmer until the birds are tender, about 30 to 40 minutes. Pour off juices, add white wine and thicken slightly with flour. Serve birds with brown rice and gravy. Number of birds depends on size of birds and your appetites.

Vegetables

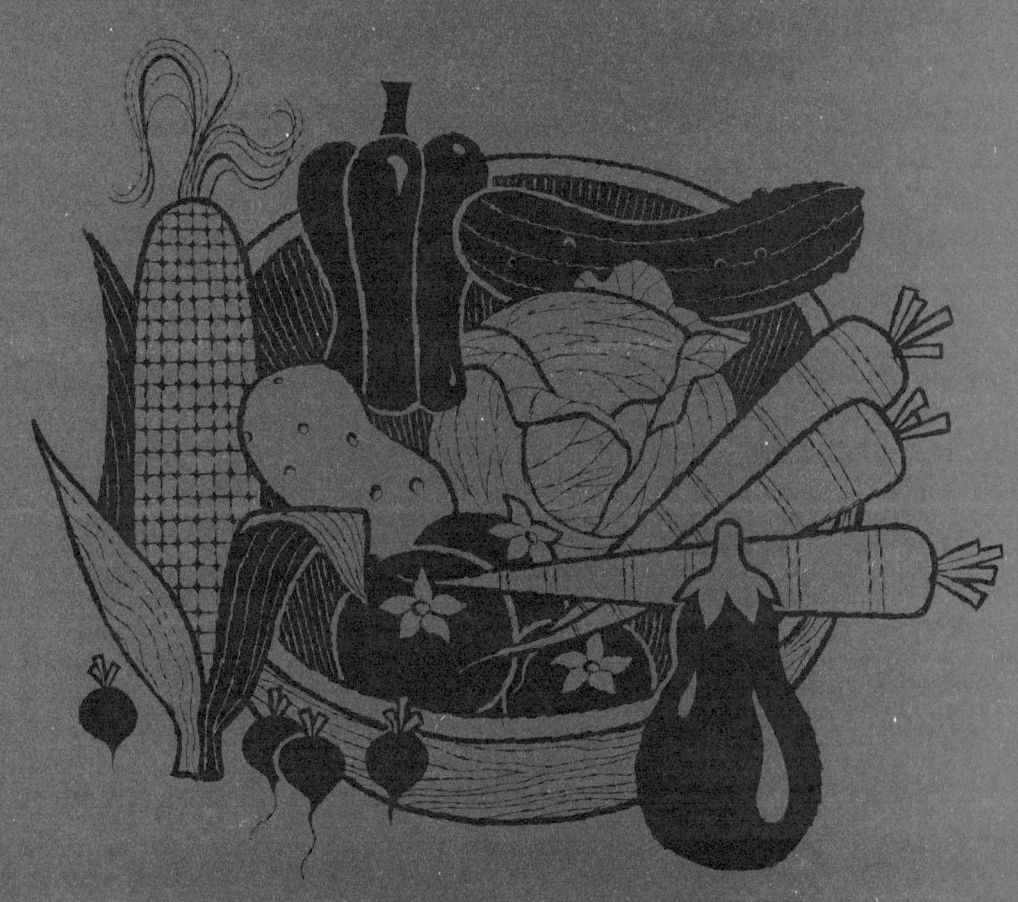

FREEZING VEGETABLES

To get the best quality frozen vegetables, freeze the freshest produce you can buy, and freeze it as quickly as possible after it is picked or purchased.

What Vegetables to Freeze

Choose vegetables your family will enjoy. Do not freeze larger quantities of items than you will want to use.

Almost any vegetable can be frozen, but some varieties of vegetables freeze better than others. Since the varieties vary from section to section of our country, write to your state extension service, experiment station or college of agriculture to get information on locally grown varieties that give highest quality when frozen.

If there is a question regarding how well a vegetable will freeze, freeze several packages and then cook it. This is only a test for freezing, not storage.

How to's With Vegetables

- When washing vegetables for freezing, always lift from the bottom, so grit will not be redistributed.
- Corn off the cob is more practical, since the cobs take precious freezer space.
- Sort vegetables according to size — unless they are to be cut into uniform pieces.
- Vegetables should be prepared for freezing in the same way as they are to be used.

Preparation for Freezing

All vegetables except green peppers should be heat treated in some manner before freezing. This slows or stops enzyme action which will cause loss of flavor and color. Heating also softens vegetables and makes them easier to pack.

Blanching is one form of heat treatment.

To blanch: Put vegetables in a wire basket. For each pound of prepared vegetables use at least 1 gallon of boiling water. Lower basket into water — put lid on blancher or kettle. Start counting time immediately. Keep heat high for time given in directions for vegetables being frozen. At 5,000 feet or more above sea level, add 1 minute.

To steam: Use a kettle with a tight lid and a rack that holds a steaming basket at least 3-inches above the bottom of the kettle. Put 1 to 2 inches of water in the kettle and bring to a boil. Put vegetables in the basket in a single layer for steam to reach all parts quickly. Cover kettle and keep heat on high. Steam according to the length of time given in the directions for vegetables being frozen. At 5,000 feet or more above sea level, add 1 minute.

Occasionally directions will be given for heating in a pressure cooker or fry pan or for simmering.

Cooling vegetables

After vegetables have been heated, they should be cooled at once to stop cooking. This can be done by:

- Plunging the basket of vegetables at once into a large quantity of 60° F. cold water (or below). Change water frequently.
- Or use cold running water.
- Or iced water. It will require about 1 pound of ice for each pound of vegetables.

When the vegetable is cooled — it takes about as long to cool as it does to heat a vegetable — remove from water and drain well.

To cool vegetables which are heated by methods other than blanching or steaming, set pan in cold water and change water frequently.

When stored at 0° F. or below, most frozen vegetables will keep good quality up to a year.

APPROXIMATE YIELD CHART

Vegetable	Fresh, As Purchased or Picked	Frozen
Asparagus	1 crate (12 2-lb. bunches)	15 to 22 pt.
	1 to 1-1/2 lb.	1 pt.
Beans, lima (in pods)	1 bu. (32 lb.)	12 to 16 pt.
	2 to 2-1/2 lb.	1 pt.
Beans, snap green, and wax	1 bu. (30 lb.)	30 to 45 pt.
	2/3 to 1 lb.	1 pt.
Beet greens	15 lb.	10 to 15 pt.
	1 to 1-1/2 lb.	1 pt.
Beets (without tops)	1 bu. (52 lb.)	35 to 42 pt.
	1-1/4 to 1-1/2 lb.	1 pt.
Broccoli	1 crate (25 lb.)	24 pt.
	1 lb.	1 pt.
Brussels sprouts	4 quart boxes	6 pt.
	1 lb.	1 pt.
Carrots (without tops)	1 bu. (50 lb.)	32 to 40 pt.
	1-1/4 to 1-1/2 lb.	1 pt.
Cauliflower	2 medium heads	3 pt.
	1-1/3 lb.	1 pt.
Chard	1 bu. (12 lb.)	8 to 12 pt.
	1 to 1-1/2 lb.	1 pt.
Collards	1 bu. (12 lb.)	8 to 12 pt.
	1 to 1-1/2 lb.	1 pt.
Corn, sweet (in husks)	1 bu. (35 lb.)	14 to 17 pt.
	2 to 2-1/2 lb.	1 pt.
Kale	1 bu. (18 lb.)	12 to 18 pt.
	1 to 1-1/2 lb.	1 pt.
Mustard greens	1 bu. (12 lb.)	8 to 12 pt.
	1 to 1-1/2 lb.	1 pt.
Peas	1 bu. (30 lb.)	12 to 15 pt.
	2 to 2-1/2 lb.	1 pt.
Peppers, sweet	2/3 lb. (3 peppers)	1 pt.
Pumpkin	3 lb.	2 pt.
Spinach	1 bu. (18 lb.)	12 to 18 pt.
	1 to 1-1/2 lb.	1 pt.
Squash, summer	1 bu. (40 lb.)	32 to 40 pt.
	1 to 1-1/4 lb.	1 pt.
Squash, winter	3 lb.	2 pt.
Sweet potatoes	2/3 lb.	1 pt.

VEGETABLES	PREPARATION
Artichokes Choose with uniform color, compact tight fitting leaves.	Remove a layer of outer leaves, wash well. Trim 1-inch off top, cut off stems. Blanch 7 minutes. Cool. Pack into containers. Leave 1/2-inch head space. Seal, label, date, freeze.
Asparagus Young tender stalks. Sort according to thickness of stalk.	Wash, cut or break off tough ends of stalks. Leave spears in lengths to fit package or cut in 2-inch pieces. Blanch small stalks 2 minutes; medium stalks 3 minutes; large stalks 4 minutes. Cool and drain. Pack into containers. When packing spears, alternate tips and stem ends. If container is wider at top than bottom, pack asparagus with tips down. Seal, label, date, freeze.
Beans, lima Beans should be green, not starchy. Shell or sort according to size.	Beans may also be blanched in pods and then shelled. Blanch small beans or pods 2 minutes; medium beans or pods 3 minutes; large beans or pods 4 minutes. Cool and drain. Shell. Pack into containers. Leave 1/2-inch head space. Seal, label, date, freeze. Note: Lima beans, shell beans, snap beans, soybeans and peas may be tray frozen if desired. Spread prepared vegetable on a metal tray. Freeze. As soon as frozen pack into freezer bags or containers. Seal, label, date, freeze.
Beans, shell, green Select plump pods, not dry or wrinkled	Wash beans thoroughly and remove ends. Cut in 1 or 2-inch lengths, or slice lengthwise for julienne beans. Blanch 3 minutes. Cool and drain. Pack into containers. Leave 1/2-inch head space. Seal, label, date, freeze.
Beans, soybeans, green Choose firm, well filled bright green pods.	Wash pods. Blanch pods 5 minutes. Cool. Squeeze soybeans out of pods. Pack into containers. Leave 1/2-inch head space. Seal, label, date, freeze.

VEGETABLES	PREPARATION
Beets Choose young or mature beets not more than 3-inches across.	Wash beets and sort according to size. Trim tops, leaving 1/2-inch stem. Cook in boiling water until tender, 25-30 minutes for small beets, 45-50 minutes for medium. Cool promptly. Peel, cut into slices or cubes. Pack into containers. Leave 1/2-inch head space. Seal, label, date, freeze.
Broccoli Select tight compact, dark green heads with tender stalks.	Wash, peel stalks and trim. To remove insects, soak for 30 minutes in a solution of 4 teaspoons salt to 1 gallon water. Split broccoli lengthwise into pieces so that heads are not more than 1-1/2-inches across. Steam 5 minutes or blanch 3 minutes. Cool and drain. Pack broccoli into containers tightly. Seal, label, date, freeze.
Brussels Sprouts Use firm, green compact heads.	Examine sprouts carefully to be sure they are free from insects. Trim to remove coarse outer leaves. Wash thoroughly. Sort into small, medium and large sizes. Blanch small sprouts 3 minutes; medium sprouts 4 minutes; large sprouts 5 minutes. Cool and drain. Pack tightly into containers. Seal, label, date, freeze.
Cabbage or Chinese Cabbage Freeze only freshly picked, solid headed cabbage.	Trim coarse, outer leaves from head. Cut into medium or large shreds or thin wedges. Bianch 1-1/2 minutes. Cool and drain. Pack cabbage into containers. Leave 1/2-inch head space. Seal, label, date, freeze. Note: Frozen cabbage, when defrosted, is suitable for cooked cabbage dishes.
Carrots Tender and mild-flavored are best for freezing.	Remove tops, wash and peel. Small carrots can be left whole. Cut others into 1/4-inch cubes, thin slices or julienne strips. Blanch whole small carrots 5 minutes; diced, sliced or julienne strips, 2 minutes. Cool and drain. Pack carrots into containers. Leave 1/2-inch head space. Seal, label, date, freeze.

VEGETABLES	PREPARATION
Cauliflower Firm, tender snow-white heads should be chosen for freezing.	Break or cut into pieces about 1-inch across. Wash well. To remove insects, soak for 30 minutes in a solution of 4 teaspoons salt to 1 gallon water. Wash well. Drain. Blanch in boiling water containing 4 teaspoons salt per gallon for 3 minutes. Cool at once and drain well. Pack tightly into containers. Seal, label, date, freeze.
Celery Freeze only crisp, tender stalks free from coarse strings.	Wash thoroughly, trim and cut into 1-inch lengths. Blanch for 3 minutes. Cool and drain. Pack into containers. Leave 1/2-inch head space. Seal, label, date, freeze.
Corn, sweet Select plump tender kerneled ears with thin sweet milk. If milk is thick and starchy, freeze corn as cream-style.	Whole kernel and Cream-style. Husk ears, remove silk and wash. Heat ears in boiling water until warm. Cool. For whole kernel corn, cut kernels from cob about 2/3 their depth. Pack into containers. Leave 1/2-inch head space. Seal, label, date, freeze. For cream-style, cut kernels at about 1/2 depth, scrape cobs with back of knife. Mix with kernels. Pack into containers. Leave 1/2-inch head space. Seal, label, date, freeze.
Corn-on-the-cob Select young tender ears with thin, sweet milk.	Remove husks, silk and wash. Sort by size. Blanch small ears 1-1/4-inch or less in diameter, 7 minutes; medium ears, 1-1/4—1-1/2-inches in diameter, 9 minutes; large ears, over 1-1/2-inch in diameter, 11 minutes. Cool and drain. Pack ears of same size into containers or wrap with freezer paper. Seal, label, date, freeze.
Eggplant Choose heavy, firm dark color eggplants	Peel and slice eggplants 1/4-inch thick. Dice or cut in strips for French fried eggplant, if desired. Dip into a solution made of 1/4 cup lemon juice or 1/2 tablespoon citric acid per quart of water about 30 seconds. Steam for 5 minutes. Cool. Pack into containers. Leave 1/2-inch head space. Seal, label, date, freeze.

**Greens,
beets, chard,
collards, kale,
mustard, spinach,
turnip.**

Select young
tender leaves.

Remove tough stems and imperfect leaves and wash well. Leaves can be left whole or cut up. Chard should be cut. Blanch 2 minutes. (Very tender leaves 1-1/2 minutes). Cool and drain. Pack into containers. Leave 1/2-inch head space. Seal, label, date, freeze.

Kohlrabi
Select young, tender, mild flavored, small to medium sized kohlrabi.

Cut off tops and roots, wash and peel. Leave whole or dice in 1/2-inch cubes. Blanch whole 3 minutes; cubes 1 minute. Cool and drain. Pack whole kohlrabi into containers or wrap in freezer paper. Seal, label, date, freeze. Pack cubes into containers. Leave 1/2-inch head space. Seal, label, date, freeze.

Mixed vegetables
Choose any combination suitable for use.

If vegetables are mixed before being blanched, blanch longest length of time indicated for the individual vegetables. Cool and drain. Pack into containers. Seal, label, date, freeze. If vegetables are blanched individually and then mixed, follow directions given for each vegetable. Cool and drain, as necessary. Mix. Pack into containers. Leave 1/2-inch head space. Seal, label, date, freeze.

Mushrooms
Select mushrooms free from spots.

Sort mushrooms according to size. Wash thoroughly and trim off ends. Mushrooms larger than 1-inch across should be cut in fourths or sliced. They may be heated in oil or steamed.
To heat in fry pan:
Heat small quantities of mushrooms in oil in an open fry pan until almost done. Cool in air—or set pan in cold water. Pack into containers. Leave 1/2-inch head space. Seal, label, date, freeze.
To steam:
Soak mushrooms in a solution containing 1-1/2 teaspoons citric acid or 1 teaspoon lemon juice to a pint of water. Drain. Steam whole mushrooms 5 minutes; buttons or quarters 3-1/2 minutes; slices 3 minutes. Cool and drain. Pack into containers. Leave 1/2-inch head space. Seal, label, date, freeze.

VEGETABLES	PREPARATION

Okra
Freeze young, tender green pods

Wash thoroughly. Cut off stems. Do not cut open seed cells. Blanch small pods 3 minutes; large pods 4 minutes. Cool and drain. Leave whole or slice crosswise. Pack into containers. Leave 1/2-inch head space. Seal, label, date, freeze.

Onions, Whole and chopped
Select small white onions or similar size for whole frozen onions. For chopped, use yellow skinned onions with no imperfections.

Whole: Wash and peel onions. Sort according to size. Cut off stem and root ends. Blanch 5 minutes. Cool. Pack into containers. Seal, label, date, freeze.
Chopped: Peel and cut off stem and root ends. Chop in pieces about 1/4-inch across. Blanch 1 minute. Cool and drain. Pack in small containers or about recipe size. Seal, label, date, freeze.
Note: Chopped onions may be tray frozen, if desired. Spread prepared onions on metal tray. Freeze. As soon as frozen, pack into freezer bags or containers. Seal, label, date.

Parsnips
Select small, tender parsnips free from woodiness.

Remove tops, wash, peel, cut into 1/2-inch cubes or slices. Blanch 2 minutes. Cool and drain. Pack into containers. Leave 1/2-inch head space. Seal, label, date, freeze.

Peas, Blackeye
Choose well filled pods.

Shell peas, discard hard peas. Blanch 2 minutes. Cool and drain. Pack into containers. Leave 1/2-inch head space. Seal, label, date, freeze.

Peas, Green
Choose bright green plump, firm pods with sweet tender peas.

Shell peas. Do not freeze immature or hard peas. Blanch 1-1/2 minutes. Cool and drain. Pack into containers. Leave 1/2-inch head space. Seal, label, date, freeze.

VEGETABLES	PREPARATION
Peppers, Sweet Choose firm, crisp, thin walled peppers.	Sweet: Wash, cut out stems, cut in half and remove seeds. If peppers are to be used for uncooked dishes such as salads, they do not need to be blanched. Blanched peppers can be used in cooked dishes, and are easier to pack. Leave in halves or 1/2-inch strips. Pack unblanched peppers in containers. Seal, label, date, freeze. Blanch halves 3 minutes; slices 2 minutes. Cool and drain. Pack into containers. Leave 1/2-inch head space. Seal, label, date, freeze.
Peppers, hot	Wash and stem peppers. Pack into small containers. Seal, label, date, freeze.
Pimientos Freeze firm, crisp, thick-walled pimientos.	To peel, roast pimientos in an oven at 400° F for 3 to 4 minutes. To remove charred skins, rinse pimientos in cold water. Drain. Pack pimientos into containers. Leave 1/2-inch head space. Seal, label, date, freeze.
Pumpkin Select full colored pumpkins with a fine texture.	Wash, cut into pieces and remove seeds. Cook pumpkin pieces until soft in boiling water, steam, pressure cooker or oven. Remove pulp from rind and mash or press through a sieve. To cool, place pan in cold water. Stir occasionally. Pack into continaers. Leave 1/2-inch head space. Seal, label, date, freeze.
Rutabagas Choose young, tender, medium size rutabagas.	Cut off tops, wash and peel. Cubed: Cut into 1/2-inch cubes. Blanch 2 minutes. Cool and drain. Pack into containers. Leave 1/2-inch head space. Seal, label, date, freeze. Mashed: Cut rutagabas in pieces and cook until tender in boiling water. Drain and mash or press through a sieve. Cool. Pack into containers. Leave 1/2-inch head space. Seal, label, date, freeze.

VEGETABLES	PREPARATION
Squash, summer Choose young squash with small seeds and tender rind.	Wash, cut in 1/2-inch slices. (Occasionally, if larger squash is used, it may be peeled before slicing). Blanch 3 minutes. Cool and drain. Pack into containers. Leave 1/2-inch head space. Seal, label, date, freeze.
Squash, winter Select firm, mature squash.	Wash, cut into pieces and remove seeds. Cook pieces until soft in boiling water, steam, pressure cooker or oven. Remove pulp from rind and mash or press through a sieve. Cool. Pack into containers. Leave 1/2-inch head space. Seal, label, date, freeze.
Sweet potatoes and Yams Choose medium to large potatoes or yams that have been treated. (Those that have been lightly waxed.)	Sweet potatoes may be packed whole, sliced or mashed. Whole: wash and sort according to size. Cook until almost tender in boiling water, steam, pressure cooker or oven. Cool and peel. Dip whole potatoes in a solution of 1 tablespoon citric acid or 1/2 cup lemon juice to 1 quart water for 5 seconds. Pack into containers. Leave 1/2-inch head space. Seal, label, date, freeze. Or pack into containers, cover with 50% syrup. Leave 1/2-inch head space. Seal, label, date, freeze. Slices: Process sweet potatoes as above. Slice. Dip slices in a solution of 1 tablespoon citric acid or 1/2 cup lemon juice to 1 quart water for 5 seconds. Pack into containers. Leave 1/2-inch head space. Seal, label, date, freeze. Or pack into containers, cover with 50% syrup. Leave 1/2-inch head space. Seal, label, date, freeze. Mashed: Process sweet potatoes as above. Mash. Pack into containers. Leave 1/2-inch head space. Seal, label, date, freeze.

VEGETABLES	PREPARATION
Tomatoes, Freeze firm, vine-ripened tomatoes.	Juice: Wash, sort and trim tomatoes. Cut into quarters and simmer 5 to 10 minutes. Press through a sieve. If desired add 1 teaspoon salt per quart. Cool. Pour into containers. Leave head space. Seal, label, date, freeze. Stewed: Remove stem ends and peel. Quarter and cook, covered, 10 to 20 minutes. Cool. Pack into containers. Leave head space. Seal, label, date, freeze. Whole: Peel whole tomatoes. Pack into a plastic bag or freezer container. Seal, label, date, freeze. Note: Frozen whole tomatoes can be used in cooking. They do not replace fresh tomatoes in salads.
Turnips Choose small firm turnips that have a mild flavor.	Wash, peel and cut into 1/2-inch cubes. Blanch 2 minutes. Cool and drain. Pack into containers. Leave 1/2-inch head space. Seal, label, date, freeze.

POINTERS ON USING FROZEN VEGETABLES

It is not necessary to thaw most frozen vegetables before cooking. Cook quickly in as small amount of water as possible in a covered saucepan. Because of the blanching, vegetables are partially pre-cooked. Some like spinach and other greens need only to be heated through to be ready to serve. If necessary, separate pieces with a fork as they begin to defrost in the water.

If corn on the cob is partially defrosted — it will heat through more quickly and avoid cooking the kernels longer than necessary.

Recipes to use food from the freezer

SWEET POTATO — BANANA PUDDING

1/2 cup raisins	1 cup frozen mashed
2 tablespoons rum	sweet potatoes, defrosted
2 eggs	1/4 teaspoon nutmeg
1/4 cup granulated sugar	1/8 teaspoon allspice
1/2 cup dark corn syrup	1/2 cup evaporated milk, heated
3 tablespoons melted buter	1 cup frozen mashed bananas,
or margarine	defrosted
1/2 teaspoon salt	

Soak raisins in rum. Beat eggs with granulated sugar until very thick. Beat in dark corn syrup and butter. Stir in remaining ingredients including raisins and rum. Pour into a well buttered 1 quart casserole. Bake at 375° F for 45 minutes or until knife comes out clean. Makes 6 servings.

Recipes to use food from the freezer

SPANISH RICE

1/4 cup bacon fat or butter	1 teaspoon chili powder
1/2 cup frozen chopped onion	1/2 teaspoon oregano
1/2 cup frozen green pepper,	2 cups frozen stewed tomatoes,
cut up	defrosted
1 pound ground beef, defrosted	1/2 cup long cooking rice
1 teaspoon salt	

Heat fat in large skillet. Saute onion, green pepper and beef until meat is lightly browned. Add remaining ingredients and mix well. Cover and cook over low heat 30 minutes or until rice is tender. Stir occasionally and add a little water, if necessary. Makes 4 servings.

STEWED TOMATOES AND OKRA

1/3 cup frozen chopped onion
1/4 cup bacon fat
1 pint frozen cut okra

1 pint frozen stewed tomatoes
1/2 teaspoon salt
Freshly ground pepper to taste

Saute onion in bacon fat until tender but not browned. Add remaining ingredients. Cover and simmer until defrosted and okra is tender, 6 to 10 minutes. Separate okra with fork when it begins to defrost. Makes 4 to 6 servings.

CAULIFLOWER POLONAISE

2 pints frozen cauliflower
1/2 cup coarse fresh bread crumbs
6 tablespoons butter
   or margarine, melted

4 teaspoons lemon juice
2 tablespoons finely
   chopped parsley

Defrost cauliflower enough to separate flowerettes and cook in a small amount of boiling, salted water until tender, 4 to 5 minutes. Drain. Saute bread crumbs in butter until lightly browned. Remove from heat and add lemon juice. Put cauliflower into a serving dish and sprinkle with crumbs and chopped parlsey. Makes 6 servings.

Fruits

FREEZING FRUITS

It is particularly rewarding to serve freezer-fresh fruits out of season for family and friends to enjoy. Freeze fruits when in their prime, to store in the freezer at 0° F. until ready for the right occasion.

What Fruits To Freeze

Fruit selections should be made on the basis of family tastes and needs, not just because some particular fruit is plentiful on your trees or a bargain at the store. Freezer space must be shared with other foods, so it is not practical to waste it on something that won't be used within a reasonable length of time.

Some fruits freeze better than others, and since the varieties vary from section to section of our country, write to your state extension service, experiment station or college of agriculture to get information on locally grown varieties that give the highest quality when frozen.

If you have doubts as to how well a fruit will freeze, it would be wise to test it before freezing large quantities. Test by freezing 3 or 4 packages and sampling the food after freezing. Remember that this shows only the effects of freezing, not storage.

How to's With Fruit

- Prepare fruit for freezing just as you would for table use. Peel and slice peaches, freeze blueberries as they come from the box.
- Fruit may be frozen in syrup pack, in sugar pack, with no sugar or tray pack. Generally speaking syrup pack fruits are used for dessert, sugar pack fruits for dessert or recipes, and fruits with no sugar for recipes or for use by persons on sugar-free diets. Tray pack fruits can be used in a variety of ways.
- Fruit to be frozen should be ripe, but not overripe. When defrosted most frozen fruits are a little softer than the fresh products. Therefore, best quality results from freezing firm ripe fruits.

General directions in preparation of fruit for the freezer.

Fruits may be packaged in rigid or non-rigid containers. Always use moisture/vapor proof freezer material and pack tight to exclude as much air as possible, except when leaving head room for liquid packs. Family size packages are preferred.

Wash all fruits before freezing. Lift from water to drain and wash fragile fruits such as berries in small quantities to avoid crushing.

Avoid using iron, galvanized ware, chipped enamel ware or poorly tinned tinware when working with fruits for freezing.

Methods of Freezing

Syrup pack: A 40% syrup is recommended for most fruits. Plan on 1/2 to 2/3 cups per pint of fruit. Syrup may be made in advance and stored in the refrigerator.

When using syrup pack be sure syrup covers fruit. Fill container with fruit to within 1-inch of top. Add syrup inserting a knife around outside of container between fruit and walls of container to be sure the syrup has gone to the bottom. Put a piece of crumpled foil or parchment paper on top of fruit to push it under syrup. Cover with lid. Seal, label, date, freeze.

Syrup Chart

	Sugar cups	Water cups	Yield of Syrup cups
30 percent syrup	2	4	5
40 percent syrup	3	4	5-1/3
60 percent syrup	7	4	7-3/4

To make syrup, dissolve sugar in cold or hot water. If hot water is used, cool syrup before using.

Sugar Pack: Cut fruit into bowl or shallow pan. Sprinkle sugar (amount as indicated in directions for each fruit) over fruit. Mix gently with a large spoon or pancake turner until sugar is dissolved and juice is drawn from fruit. Pack into containers and put a piece of crumpled foil or parchment paper on top of fruit to push it under juice. Cover with lid. Seal, label, date, freeze.

Unsweetened or Dry Pack: Pack prepared fruit in containers without adding liquid or sweetening, or crush fruit and pack in its own liquid. Press fruit into juice with crumpled foil or parchment paper. Close and seal containers, label, date, freeze.

Label all containers with amount of sugar (or no sugar) and sweetness of syrup for aid in using fruit in recipes when defrosted.

To keep fruits from darkening.

If not treated, some fruits may darken during freezing.

Ascorbic acid, also known as Vitaminc C, is the most efficient product to use to keep fruits from darkening. It also enhances the flavor and adds to the nutritive value. It is easier to use if purchased in crystalline form which is sold in most stores that carry freezer supplies. However, drug stores have Vitamin C in tablet form, labeled as to the milligrams per tablet. Tablets contain a filler which may make syrup slightly cloudy when they are dissolved, but this does not affect quality.

In order to translate crystalline ascorbic acid into its equivalent in tablets, use this table.

Crystalline Ascorbic Acid	Ascorbic Acid Tablets
1/8 teaspoon	375 milligrams
1/4 teaspoon	750 milligrams
1/2 teaspoon	1,500 milligrams
3/4 teaspoon	2,250 milligrams
1 teaspoon	3,000 milligrams

To use ascorbic acid, dissolve in a little cold water. Crush tablets so they will dissolve more easily. Keep refrigerated and make up as needed.

In syrup pack. Gently stir dissolved ascorbic acid into cold syrup.

In sugar pack. Sprinkle dissolved ascorbic acid over fruit just before adding sugar.

In unsweetened pack. Sprinkle dissolved ascorbic acid over fruit and mix thoroughly before packing into containers.

In fruit juices. Add ascorbic acid directly to juice. Stir only enough to dissolve ascorbic acid.

In crushed fruit and fruit purees. Add dissolved ascorbic acid to fruit and mix.

There are also commercial products such as Fruit-Fresh available to prevent darkening. They are usually a combination of ascorbic acid, sugar and filler. They should be used according to the directions on the package.

APPROXIMATE YIELD CHART

Fruit	Fresh, as Purchased or Picked	Frozen
Apples	1 bu. (48 lb.)	32 to 40 pt.
	1 box (44 lb.)	29 to 35 pt.
	1-1/4 to 1-1/2 lb.	1 pt.
Apricots	1 bu. (48 lb.)	60 to 72 pt.
	1 crate (22 lb.)	28 to 33 pt.
	2/3 to 4/5 lb.	1 pt.
Berries[1]	1 crate (24 qt.)	32 to 36 pt.
	1-1/3 to 1-1/2 pt.	1 pt.
Cantaloupes	1 dozen (28 lb.)	22 pt.
	1 to 1-1/4 lb.	1 pt.
Cherries, sweet or sour	1 bu. (56 lb.)	36 to 44 pt.
	1-1/4 to 1-1/2 lb.	1 pt.
Cranberries	1 box (25 lb.)	50 pt.
	1 peck (8 lb.)	16 pt.
	1/2 lb.	1 pt.
Currants	2 qt. (3 lb.)	4 pt.
	3/4 lb.	1 pt.
Peaches	1 bu. (48 lb.)	32 to 48 pt.
	1 lug box (20 lb.)	13 to 20 pt.
	1 to 1-1/2 lb.	1 pt.
Pears	1 bu. (50 lb.)	40 to 50 pt.
	1 western box (46 lb.)	37 to 46 pt.
	1 to 1-1/2 lb.	1 pt.
Pineapple	5 lb.	4 pt.
Plums and prunes	1 bu. (56 lb.)	38 to 56 pt.
	1 crate (20 lb.)	13 to 20 pt.
	1 to 1-1/2 lb.	1 pt.
Raspberries	1 crate (24 pt.)	24 pt.
	1 pt.	1 pt.
Rhubarb	15 lb.	15 to 22 pt.
	2/3 to 1 lb.	1 pt.
Strawberries	1 crate (24 qt.)	38 pt.
	2/3 qt.	1 pt.

[1] Includes blackberries, blueberries, boysenberries, dewberries, elderberries, gooseberries, huckleberries, loganberries and youngberries.

Apples

Select full-flavored crisp and firm apples. Wash, peel and core. Slice medium size into 12ths, large into 16ths. Pack.

Syrup: 40% syrup with 1/2 teaspoon crystalline ascorbic acid to each quart syrup. Slice apples directly into cold syrup in container. Press fruit into syrup. Leave head space. Seal, label, date, freeze.

Fruit cocktail, uncooked, dessert, salads

Sugar: To prevent darkening slice apples into solution of 2 tablespoons salt to 1 gallon water. Do not hold in this solution more than 15-20 minutes. Drain. To retard darkening, place layers in single layer in steamer. Steam 1-1/2 to 2 minutes. Cool in cold water. Over each quart sprinkle 1/2 cup sugar and stir. Pack into containers. Leave head space. Seal, label, date, freeze.

Pies, cobblers, etc.

Unsweetened: follow directions for sugar pack except omit sugar.

Sauce: Select full flavored apples. Wash, quarter. Add 1/3 cup water to each quart apples. Cook, covered, until tender. Strain. Sweeten to taste. Cool. Pack into containers leaving head space. Seal, label, date, freeze.

Dessert, recipes calling for apple sauce.

Apricots

Select firm, ripe, uniformly yellow apricots. Sort, wash, halve and pit. Peel and slice, if desired.

Syrup: 40% syrup with 3/4 teaspoon crystalline ascorbic acid to each quart syrup. Pack apricots directly into container. Cover with syrup, leaving head space. Seal, label, date, freeze.

Serve as is, in salads

Sugar: Dissolve 1/4 teaspoon crystalline ascorbic acid in 1/4 cup cold water. Sprinkle over 1 quart of fruit. Mix 1/2 cup sugar with each quart of fruit. Stir until sugar is dissolved. Pack apricots into containers. Press down to cover fruit with juice, leaving head space. Seal, label, date, freeze.

Pies, other cooked dishes

Crushed or Puree: Select fully ripe fruit. Dip in boiling water, 1/2 minute, cool in cold water. Peel apricots. Pit and crush coarsely or put through sieve or puree in blender. Add 1 cup sugar and 1/4 teaspoon crystalline ascorbic acid dissolved in 1/4 cup water to each quart. Pack in containers, leaving head space. Seal, label, date, freeze.

Use for cooked dishes or gelatines or to make jams.

FRUIT	TYPE OF PACK	USE
Avocados 2 to 3 avocados depending on size, per pint.	Select avocados that are softripe, rinds free from dark blemishes. Peel, remove pit, mash fruit.	
	Unsweetened: Add 1/8 teaspoon crystalline ascorbic acid to each quart puree. Mix well. Pack into containers leaving head space. Seal, label, date, freeze.	Salads, sandwiches, guacamole
	Sugar: Mix 1 cup sugar and 1/8 teaspoon crystalline ascorbic acid to each quart puree. Pack into containers leaving head space. Seal, label, date, freeze.	Ice Cream, milkshakes, desserts
Bananas 2 large per pint	Select ripe bananas. Peel and mash. Mix 1/4 teaspoon crystalline ascorbic acid dissolved in 1 tablespoon water to each cup. Pack in containers. Leave head space. Seal, label, date, freeze.	For banana bread or other baked recipes
Berries **(black,** **boysen,** **dew, logan** **young)**	Select firm, plump, fully ripe berries with glossy skins. Avoid green berries. Sort and remove any leaves and stems. Wash and drain.	
	Syrup: Pack berries into containers and cover with cold 40% syrup. Leave head space. Seal, label, date, freeze.	Uncooked dessert
	Sugar: To 1 quart berries, add 3/4 cup sugar. Gently mix berries with sugar until dissolved. Fill containers, leaving head space. Seal, label, date, freeze.	Cooked dishes
	Unsweetened: Pack berries into containers, leaving head space. Seal, label, date, freeze.	Diets
	Crushed or puree: Crush or press washed and hulled berries through a sieve. To each quart add 1 cup sugar, stirring until sugar is dissolved. Pack into containers, leaving head space. Seal, label, date, freeze.	Cooked dishes, jam.
	Note: All berries can be tray frozen, if desired. Spread prepared berries on metal tray. Freeze. As soon as frozen, pack into freezer bags or containers. Seal, label, date, freeze.	

FRUIT	TYPE OF PACK	USE
Berries (blue, elder, huckle)	Select full flavored, ripe berries all about the same size, preferably with tender skins. Sort, wash and drain. If desired, steam for 1 minute and cool immediately. This tenderizes skin.	
	Syrup: Pack berries into containers and cover with cold 40% syrup. Leave head space. Seal, label, date, freeze.	To serve uncooked, as dessert on cereal
	Unsweetened: Pack berries into containers. Leave head space. Seal, label, date, freeze.	Cooking, diets
	Crushed or Puree: Select fully ripened berries. Sort, wash and drain. Crush or press berries through fine sieve for puree. To 1 quart, add 1 cup sugar. Stir until sugar is dissolved. Pack into containers. Leave head space. Seal, label, date, freeze.	Jams or recipes
Cherries, sour	Select bright red, tree ripened cherries. Stem, sort and wash thoroughly. Drain and pit.	
	Syrup: Pack cherries into containers and cover with 60% syrup. Leave head space. Seal, label, date, freeze.	Sauce, salads, recipes
	Sugar: To 1 quart cherries add 3/4 cup sugar. Mix until sugar is dissolved. Pack into containers. Leave head space. Seal, label, date, freeze.	Pies or other cooked products
	Crushed: Crush prepared cherries coarsely. To 1 quart add about 1-1/2 cups sugar. Mix until sugar is dissolved. Pack into containers. Leave head space. Seal, label, date, freeze.	Recipes or jam
	Puree: Crush prepared cherries or puree in blender, heat to boiling, cool and press through a sieve. To 1 quart add 3/4 cup sugar. Pack into containers. Leave head space. Seal, label, date, freeze.	Recipes or jam
	Juice: Crush prepared cherries. Heat slightly, put into jelly bag, let hang overnight. Pour off clear juice for freezing or pack juice and strain when defrosted. Sweeten to taste or freeze without sugar. Pour into containers. Leave head space. Seal, label, date, freeze.	Jelly or juice for punches

FRUIT	TYPE OF PACK	USE

Cherries, sweet

Select well colored, tree ripened fruit with a sweet flavor. Sort, stem, wash and drain. Remove pits, if desired. If left in they tend to give an almond like flavor to the cherries.

Whole: Work quickly to avoid color and flavor change. Pack into containers. Cover with 40% syrup with 1/2 teaspoon crystalline ascorbic acid per quart. Leave head space. Seal, label, date, freeze.

Desserts, in salads

Crushed: Prepare cherries, remove pits. Crush. To each quart (2 pounds) crushed fruit, add 1-1/2 cups sugar and 1/4 teaspoon crystalline ascorbic acid. Mix well. Pack into containers. Leave head space. Seal, label, date, freeze.

Jams desserts

Juice: Crush prepared cherries. Heat slightly. Put into jelly bag. Let hang overnight. Pour off clear juice for freezing or freeze all juice and strain when defrosted. Sweeten to taste, or freeze, unsweetened. Put into containers. Leave head space. Seal, label, date, freeze.

Jellies or juice for punches

Note 1: A combination of half sweet and half sour cherry juice can be frozen for a less sweet product.

Note 2: Extract white cherry juice without heating. Then heat over low heat.

Coconut, fresh

Reserve coconut milk. Chop white meat of coconut in blender or food chopper. Pack in containers with coconut milk. Leave head space. Seal, label, date, freeze.

Baking, desserts, salads

Cranberries

Select firm, deep red berries with glossy skin. Stem, wash and drain.

Whole, unsweetened: Pack into containers without sugar. Seal, label, date, freeze.

Whole, sweetened: Pack berries into containers. Cover with cold 40% syrup. Leave head space. Seal, label, date, freeze.

For sauce or recipes

Puree: Add 2 cups water to each quart (1 pound) prepared berries. Cook until skins pop. Press through a sieve. Add sugar to taste. Pack into containers. Leave head space. Seal, label, date, freeze.

For jelly or recipes

FRUIT	TYPE OF PACK	USE
Cranberries	**Note:** Cranberries can be tray frozen. Spread prepared berries on metal tray. Freeze. As soon as frozen, pack into plastic bags or containers. Seal, label, date, freeze.	
Currants	Select fully ripe, plump, bright red currants. Wash in cold water and remove stems. Drain.	
	Unsweetened: Pack into containers. Leave head space. Seal label, date, freeze.	
	Syrup: Pack currants into containers and cover with 40% syrup. Leave head space. Seal, label, date, freeze.	Dessert or recipes
	Sugar: Add 3/4 cup sugar to each quart of fruit. Stir until sugar is dissolved. Pack into containers. Leave head space. Seal, label, date, freeze.	
	Crushed: Crush prepared fruit. Add 1 cup sugar to each quart crushed fruit. Stir until sugar is dissolved. Pack into containers. Leave head space. Seal, label, date, freeze.	Jam
	Juice: For juice choose ripe currants. For jelly making mix ripe with slightly underripe. Crush prepared currants and warm over low heat. Do not boil. Press warm fruit in jelly bag to extract juice. Cool. Sweeten to taste or freeze without sugar. Pour into containers. Leave head space. Seal, label, date, freeze.	Jelly or beverages
Dates	Select dates with good flavor and tender texture. Wash and slit to remove pits. Leave whole or press through a sieve to puree. Pack into containers. Leave head space. Seal, label, date, freeze.	Desserts candies baked goods
Figs 1 pound per pint	Select tree-ripened figs that are soft ripe. Make sure figs do not have sour centers. Sort, wash, cut off stems. Peel if desired. Slice or leave whole.	
	Syrup: Pack figs into containers. Cover with 30% syrup with 3/4 teaspoon crystalline ascorbic acid added to each quart of syrup. Leave head space. Seal, label, date, freeze.	Desserts, salads, recipes
	Unsweetened: Pack figs into containers. Leave head space. Seal, label, date, freeze.	Diets

FRUIT	TYPE OF PACK	USE
Figs 1 pound per pint	**Crushed:** Crush prepared figs coarsely. To each quart, mix in 2/3 cup sugar and 1/4 teaspoon crystalline ascorbic acid. Pack into containers. Leave head space. Seal, label, date, freeze.	Jam, baked goods
Fruit cocktail	Use any combination of fruit. Sliced or cubed peaches, apricots, melon balls, sweet cherries, pineapple, orange or grapefruit sections. Pack fruit into containers. Cover with 30%syrup to which 1/2 teaspoon crystalline ascorbic acid has been added per quart of syrup. Leave head space. Seal, label, date, freeze.	First course, desserts, in gelatin
Gooseberries 1-1/3 to 1-1/2 pounds per pint	Choose fully ripe berries if being frozen for pie, underripe for jelly making. Sort, remove stems and blossom ends, wash and drain. **Unsweetened:** Pack fruit into containers. Leave head space. Seal, label, date, freeze. **Sweetened:** Pack into containers. Cover with 60% syrup. Leave head space. Seal, label, date, freeze.	Pies, jelly
Grapefruit, **Oranges**	Select firm, tree-ripened grapefruit, heavy for its size and no soft spots. Wash and peel. Cut sections away from membrane and remove seeds. Oranges may be either sectioned or sliced, after peeling. **Syrup:** Pack fruit into containers. Cover with 40% syrup made using all or part grapefruit juice from preparation. Add 1/2 teaspoon crystalline ascorbic acid to each quart of syrup. Leave head space. Seal, label, date, freeze. **Juice:** Extract juice being careful not to press oil from rind. Sweeten with 1/2 cup sugar per gallon of juice and add 3/4 teaspoon crystalline ascorbic acid per gallon. Leave head space. Seal, label, date, freeze.	Salads, sauce Punch, recipes
Grapes	Select firm ripe grapes with tender skins, full flavor and color. Wash and stem. Leave seedless grapes whole. Cut table grapes in half and remove seeds. Grapes are best frozen in syrup. Grapes for jelly may be frozen unsweetened.	Use depends on type of grape

FRUIT	TYPE OF PACK	USE
Grapes	**Unsweetened:** Pack prepared grapes into containers. Leave head space. Seal, label, date, freeze.	Table grapes, sauce, salad recipes
	Syrup: Pack prepared grapes into containers. Cover with 40% syrup. Leave head space. Seal, label, date, freeze.	Concord grapes, jelly, juice, jam
	Puree: Heat prepared grapes to boiling. (No need to remove seeds). Drain off juice. Cool and package. Leave head space. Seal, label, date, freeze.	
	Cool crushed grapes and put them through a sieve. To 1 quart puree add 1/2 cup sugar. Leave head space. Seal, label, date, freeze.	
	Note: If puree developes a gritty texture from tartrate crystals, do not be alarmed. They will dissolve when puree is heated.	
	Juice: For beverage juice, select as for whole grapes. For jelly, select grapes as suggested in jelly recipe. Wash, stem and crush grapes. Strain through a jelly bag. Let juice stand overnight in refrigerator to allow sediment to sink to bottom. Pour off clear juice into containers. Leave head room. Seal, label, date, freeze. If tartrate crystals form in frozen juice, remove by straining thawed juice.	Beverage or jelly
Melons **Cantaloupe** **Crenshaw** **Honeydew** **Persian** **Watermelon** 1 to 1-1/4 pounds per pint	Select firm, well flavored, well colored ripe melon. Cut melons in half, remove seeds and peel. Cut into slices, cubes or balls. **Syrup:** Pack prepared melon into containers. Cover with 30% syrup. Leave head space. Seal, label, date, freeze.	Sauce or salads
Nectarines 1 to 1-1/2 pounds per pint	Choose fully ripe, well-colored, firm nectarines. Do not use overripe fruit. Peel if desired. **Syrup:** Cut fruit directly into cold 40% syrup to which 1/2 teaspoon crystalline ascorbic acid has been added per quart. Start with about 1/2 cup for each pint containers. Press fruit down. Add syrup to cover. Leave head space. Seal, label, date, freeze.	Sauce, recipes, and salads

FRUIT	TYPE OF PACK	USE

Peaches Select firm, ripe peaches with no green color or skin. Sort, wash, pit and peel. A better product is produced if peaches are **not** peeled with a boiling water dip.

Syrup: Cut peaches directly into cold 40% syrup to which 1/2 teaspoon crystalline ascorbic acid has been added per quart. Start with about 1/2 cup syrup for each pint container. Press fruit down. Add syrup to cover. Leave head space. Seal, label, date, freeze.

Sauce, recipes salads

Sugar: Sprinkle 1/4 teaspoon crystalline ascorbic acid dissolved in 1/4 cup cold water over each quart prepared peaches. Add 2/3 cup sugar and mix well. Pack into containers. Leave head space. Seal, label, date, freeze.

Sauce, recipes

Water: Pack peaches into containers. Mix 1 teaspoon crystalline ascorbic acid with 1 quart cold water. Pour over peaches. Leave head space. Seal, label, date, freeze.

Recipes, diet menus

Crushed or puree: To loosen skins, dip peaches in boiling water 1/2 to 1 minute. Cool in cold water. Remove skins and pit. Crush peaches coarsely, or to puree. Press through a sieve or puree in the blender. Mix 1 cup sugar and 1/8 teaspoon crystalline ascorbic acid to each quart crushed or pureed peaches. Pack into containers. Leave head space. Seal, label, date, freeze.

Jam

Pears Select well ripened pears, that are firm but not hard. Wash, peel, cut in halves or quarters and core.

Syrup: Heat pears in boiling 40% syrup for 1 to 2 minutes depending on size of fruit. Drain and cool. Pack in containers. Cover with 40% syrup to which 3/4 teaspoon crystalline ascorbic acid has been added per quart syrup. Leave head space. Seal, label, date, freeze.

Sauce, salads, recipes

Puree: Select well ripened pears, not hard or gritty. Peel and core. Put through a sieve or puree in blender. Add 1 cup sugar and 1/8 teaspoon crystalline ascorbic acid and mix well. Pack into containers. Leave head space. Seal, label, date, freeze.

Jams, gelatin salads, fruit fillings

FRUIT	TYPE OF PACK	USE
Persimmons 1-1/4 to 1-1/2 pounds per pint	Select orange colored soft-ripe persimmons. Sort, wash, peel and cut into sections. Press through a sieve. Add 1/8 teaspoon crystalline ascorbic acid or 1-1/2 teaspoons crystalline citric acid. Sweeten to taste or pack unsweetened. Pack into containers. Leave head space. Seal, label, date, freeze.	Jams or in recipes
Pineapples	Select firm, ripe pineapples with full flavor and aroma. In choosing pineapple, pull out a leaf. If it comes out easily, the pineapple may be assumed to be ripe or nearly so. Peel and core. Then slice, dice, crush or cut pineapple into wedges.	
	Unsweetened: Pack fruit into containers, pressing tightly into containers. Leave head space.	Recipes
	Syrup: Pack fruit tightly into containers. Cover with 30% syrup made with pineapple juice, if available, or water. Leave head space. Seal, label, date, freeze.	Sauce, recipes
Plums, Prunes	Select firm tree-ripened fruit with a deep color. Sort and wash. Leave whole or cut in halves or quarters.	
	Unsweetened: Pack whole fruit into containers. Leave head space. Seal, label, date, freeze. To serve uncooked, dip frozen plums in cold water 5 to 10 seconds. Remove skins. Cover with 40% syrup to thaw.	Sauce, salads, pies or recipes
	Syrup: Pack cut fruit into containers and cover with 40% syrup to which 1/2 teaspoon crystalline ascorbic acid has been added per quart syrup. Leave head space. Seal, label, date, freeze.	Use for salads, sauces, recipes
	Puree: Use fully ripe fruit. Cut in half, remove seeds. Add 1 cup water to 4 quarts fruit. Bring to a boil, cook 2 minutes. Cool. Press through sieve. Sweeten to taste. Pack into containers. Leave head space. Seal, label, date, freeze.	Jams and fruit fillings
	Juice: For beverage juice, use fully ripe fruit. For jelly, select plums as suggested in jelly recipe. Wash plums, simmer until soft in just enough water to cover. Strain through a jelly bag. Cool. Pour into containers. Leave head space. Seal, label, date, freeze.	Beverage, jelly

FRUIT	TYPE OF PACK	USE

Raspberries
1 pint for
1 pint

Select fully ripe, juicy berries. Sort, wash carefully in cold water and drain thoroughly.

Sugar: To 1 quart berries (1-1/3 pounds) add 3/4 cup sugar. Mix carefully to avoid crushing. Spoon into containers. Leave head space. Seal, label, date, freeze. — Sauce or recipes

Syrup: Put prepared berries into containers. Cover with 40% syrup. Leave head space. Seal, label, date, freeze.

Unsweetened: Put prepared berries into containers. Leave head space. Seal, label, date, freeze.

Note: Raspberries can be tray frozen, if desired. Spread prepared berries on metal tray. Freeze. As soon as frozen, pack into plastic bags or containers. Seal, label, date, freeze.

Crushed or Puree: Crush prepared berries or puree through a sieve. Add 3/4 to 1 cup sugar per quart. Mix until sugar is dissolved. Spoon into containers. Leave head space. Seal, label, date, freeze. — Jam or recipes

Juice: For beverage, use ripe berries. For jelly select berries as suggested in jelly recipe. Crush and heat berries slightly to start flow of juice. Strain in a jelly bag to extract juice. Pour into containers. Leave head space. Seal, label, date, freeze. — Beverage, jelly

Rhubarb

Stalks should be firm, tender, well colored, have good flavor and few fibers. Wash, trim and cut into 1 to 2-inch pieces. Blanch rhubarb in boiling water for 1 minute. Drain and cool at once in cold water. This helps retain color and flavor.

Unsweetened: Pack prepared rhubarb tightly in containers. Leave head space. Seal label, date, freeze. — Pies, sauce recipes

Syrup pack: Pack prepared rhubarb tightly in containers. Cover with 40% syrup. Leave head space. Seal, label, date, freeze. — Sauce, pies

Puree: Prepare rhubarb, except omit blanching. Add 1 cup water to each 1-1/2 quarts cut rhubarb, and boil 2 minutes. Cool and press through sieve. Mix 2/3 cup sugar to each quart. Cool. Spoon into containers. Leave head space. Seal, label, date, freeze. — Jam or recipes

FRUIT	TYPE OF PACK	USE
Rhubarb	**Juice:** Cut washed rhubarb into pieces 4 to 6 inches long. Add 1 quart water to 4 quarts rhubarb. Bring just to a boil. Press hot rhubarb in jelly bag to extract juice. Cool. Pour into containers. Leave head space. Seal, label, date, freeze.	Jelly or beverage
Strawberries	Choose firm, ripe berries with a slightly tart flavor. Use larger berries for sliced or crushed. Sort and wash berries in cold water. Drain well and remove hulls. **Syrup:** Put prepared berries in containers. Cover with 40% syrup. Leave head space. Seal, label, date, freeze.	
	Sugar: Add 3/4 cup sugar to 1 quart prepared berries. Mix thoroughly. Pack into containers. Leave head space. Seal, label, date, freeze.	Sauce, recipes
	Unsweetened: Pack prepared berries into containers. Leave head space. If desired, for better color, cover berries with water mixed with 1 teaspoon crystalline ascorbic acid per quart water.	Dietetic or recipes
	Sliced or crushed: Prepare berries as directed. Slice or crush. Mix 3/4 cup sugar to each quart berries. Pack into containers. Leave head space. Seal, label, date, freeze.	Jam, recipes
	Puree: Puree prepared berries through sieve. Add 2/3 cup sugar to each quart puree. Spoon into containers. Leave head space. Seal, label, date, freeze.	Jam
	Juice: Crush prepared berries and strain through jelly bag. Add 2/3 cup sugar to each quart juice, or leave unsweetened. Pour into containers. Leave head space. Seal, label, date, freeze.	
	Note: Strawberries may be tray frozen, if desired. Spread prepared berries on metal tray. Freeze. As soon as frozen, pack into plastic bags or containers. Seal, label, date, freeze. Tray pack frozen berries lose some color during storage.	

POINTERS ON USING FROZEN FRUITS

If frozen fruits are to be served raw they should be thawed enough to separate pieces. Serve with a little ice still in the fruit for best flavor and texture.

To retain flavor and color let fruit defrost in package either in the refrigerator, at room temperature or in a pan of cool water.

For refrigerator defrosting allow 6 to 8 hours for a 1 pound package of fruit in syrup. A little longer for both fruits in sugar and unsweetened. If there is left-over fruit, it will keep better if cooked.

To cook frozen fruits, defrost enough to separate pieces. Then cook with additional sugar if needed according to type of pack, and enough water to prevent from sticking to pan.

For use in recipes, defrost and proceed with recipe.

Recipes to use food from the freezer

APPLE SAUCE VARIATIONS

- To 1 pint defrosted, sweetened apple sauce, add 2 tablespoons finely chopped fresh mint.

- To 1 pint defrosted, sweetened applesauce add 1/2 teaspoon ground nutmeg and 2 tablespoons prepared horseradish. Good as a relish with ham, pork or lamb.

- Mix 1 pint defrosted, sweetened applesauce with 1 cup defrosted crushed pineapple. Serve topped with sour cream.

- Add 1/2 teaspoon cinnamon, 1/4 teaspoon nutmeg and 1/4 cup raisins to 1 pint defrosted, sweetened applesauce. Use as a topping for cereal.

Recipes to use food from the freezer

COCONUT CAKE

2 cups cake flour	3 eggs
2-1/2 teaspoons baking powder	1 teaspoon vanilla extract
1/2 teaspoon salt	1 cup chopped coconut,
2/3 cup shortening	defrosted
1 cup sugar	2/3 cup milk

Sift together flour, baking powder and salt. Set aside. Cream shortening. Gradually add sugar and cream until light. Beat in eggs. Add vanilla and coconut. Add dry sifted ingredients alternately with milk, stirring just enough to blend. Spoon into two greased and floured 8-inch round cake pans. Bake at 375° F. 20-25 minutes. Let cool on rack 5 minutes and carefully remove from pans. Cool on rack. Frost with Fluffy White Frosting.

PEARS LUCILLE

2 pints frozen sliced pears
   in syrup, defrosted
1 tablespoon cornstarch
2 tablespoons orange juice
2 teaspoons grated
   orange rind
1 egg

1/2 cup sugar
2 tablespoons flour
1 teaspoon baking powder
1/8 teaspoon each salt,
   nutmeg and ginger
1/4 teaspoon almond extract
1/4 cup chopped almonds

Drain juice from pears and reserve. Arrange pears in bottom of greased 8 x 8 x 2-inch square baking pan. Mix juice with cornstarch, orange juice and grated orange rind. Pour over pears. Beat egg and sugar together until light. Fold in flour, baking powder, salt, spices, and almond extract. Pour over pears. Sprinkle with nuts. Bake at 325° F for 40-45 minutes or until lightly browned. Serve warm or cold. Makes 6 servings.

PRUNE WHIP

2 egg whites
1/4 teaspoon salt
4 tablespoons sugar

2 tablespoons lemon juice
1-1/2 cups frozen
   pureed prunes, defrosted

Whip egg whites with salt until stiff. Gradually beat in the sugar. Beat in lemon juice and prune puree until mixture is very fluffy. Pile lightly in individual serving dishes and chill. Makes 4 servings.

PINEAPPLE LOVELY

1 cup frozen, crushed
    pineapple, defrosted
8 large marshmallows, diced
1 cup crushed vanilla
    wafers

1 cup frozen dates, defrosted,
    chopped
1/4 cup chopped coconut,
    defrosted
2/3 cup heavy cream, whipped

Drain pineapple. (Use the juice with orange juice for breakfast). Mix pineapple lightly with remaining ingredients. Chill thoroughly. Serve with additional whipped cream, if desired. Makes 6 to 8 servings.

SPICY SHORTCAKE FOR FRUIT

2 cups all purpose flour
1 teaspoon salt
4 tablespoons sugar
1 tablespoon baking powder
1/2 teaspoon nutmeg

1/4 teaspoon cinnamon
1/3 cup shortening
2/3 cup milk (approximate)
Softened butter or margarine
Defrosted fruit

Mix flour with remaining dry ingredients in a bowl. Cut in shortening with a pastry blender or 2 knives until well blended. Stir in enough milk with a fork to make a soft dough. Pat out on a floured board 1/4 inch thick. Cut 12 3 to 4-inch rounds. Spread six rounds with softened butter and top each with the remaining pieces. Bake on a cookie sheet at 425° F 12-15 minutes or until nicely browned. Split and serve with just defrosted fruits between and on top. Makes 6 servings. Good with peaches, sweet cherries, berries, apricots.

Recipes to use food from the freezer

PEACH AND RASPBERRY COMPOTE

2 cups frozen cut up peaches
1 cup frozen red raspberries
Sugar to taste

1 tablespoon lemon juice
1/2 cup cream, whipped or
1/2 pint softened
    vanilla ice cream

Allow peaches and raspberries to defrost just enough to separate. Add sugar to taste, if needed, and lemon juice and stir lightly to mix. Spoon into 4 or 5 compote dishes. Top with whipped cream or softened vanilla ice cream.

Recipes to use food from the freezer

BLUEBERRY BETTY

2 cups frozen blueberries
1/2 cup sugar
1/4 cup water
Dash salt

1 tablespoon lemon juice
2 cups cornflakes
1/4 teaspoon cinnamon
2 tablespoons butter
    or margarine

Butter a 5 or 6-cup baking dish.

Combine blueberries with sugar, water, salt and lemon juice and simmer, covered, 5 minutes. Spoon half the blueberry mixture into the baking dish. Top with 1 cup cornflakes, coarsely crushed. Spoon in remaining blueberries and crush remaining cornflakes over them. Drizzle with cinnamon and butter. Bake at 375° F. for 25 minutes. Serve warm with Dairy sour cream. Makes 4 servings.

STRAWBERRY PUDDING

1 quart strawberries	1 cup heavy cream
1 cup sugar	1/4 cup confectioners sugar
1 cup milk	1/2 teaspoon vanilla
1 tablespoon lemon juice	1 cup vanilla cake crumbs

Wash berries and hull. Place in a bowl and crush slightly. Add sugar, cover and let stand 2 hours. Mix in milk and lemon juice and spoon into a 2-quart aluminum mold. Whip cream until stiff. Fold in sugar, vanilla and crumbs. Spoon over strawberries. Cover and freeze. Seal, label and date.

Storage time: 6 months.

To use: Remove cover, dip mold in warm water and invert on a chilled platter. Garnish with fresh strawberries, if desired. Let set in refrigerator 30 minutes before serving. Makes 8 servings.

Breads and Rolls

BREADS AND ROLLS

Breads can be baked, cooled and then frozen, or they can be prepared, frozen and then baked. This section contains recipes for both. Recipes for freezing the dough are specially developed, so do not try to freeze the dough of a recipe which is not specifically designed for freezing. The freezer is a wonderful place to store bread. Even if for only a day or two, the freezer is better than the refrigerator because it retards drying out and loss of flavor.

How to's With Bread

- "Store bought" bread can be frozen, but it should be rewrapped in moisture/vapor-proof freezer wrap.
- Breads can be cut more easily when partially defrosted.
- Slice and butter French bread and wrap in aluminum foil to freeze. It can go from freezer to oven to heat. Allow 10 to 15 minutes longer heating time.
- Purchased sweet breads that are frosted should be first frozen unwrapped and then wrapped and returned to freezer. If you are making them at home, frost after they come from the freezer.
- If you are going to make much homemade bread, buy a good bread knife.
- Rolls can be put into freezer bags for freezing. It is easy then to take out the number needed for a meal, retie the bag and return to the freezer.
- Follow the recipe. Making your own changes in bread recipes is likely to result in an inferior product.
- To make a warm place for the bread to rise, put a bowl of boiling hot water in the oven with the bread. In a gas oven with a pilot light there may be enough warmth. Or if an oven has a light, turn that on as a source of heat.
- Hot water means very hot tap water — 120 to 130° F. It should feel hot to your wrist.
- To test when bread is done, lightly tap loaf with finger. Fully baked bread should sound hollow.

Storage Time for Breads

Yeast breads and rolls .... 6 months
Yeast sweet breads .... 6 months
Yeast frozen dough .... 4 weeks
Quick breads (baking powder) .... 6 months

CRACKED WHEAT BREAD

4-3/4 to 5-3/4 cups all purpose flour	1-1/2 cups water
3 tablespoons sugar	1/2 cup milk
4 teaspoons salt	3 tablespoons margarine
3 packages active dry yeast	1 cup cracked wheat (bulgar)

In a large bowl thoroughly mix 2 cups flour, sugar, salt and undissolved yeast. Combine water, milk and margarine in a saucepan. Heat over low heat until liquids are very warm (120° F. to 130° F.). Margarine does not need to melt. Gradually add to dry ingredients and beat for 2 minutes at medium speed of electric mixer, scraping bowl occasionally. Add cracked wheat and beat at high speed for 2 minutes, scraping bowl occasionally. Stir in enough additional flour to make a stiff dough. Turn out onto lightly floured board; knead until smooth and elastic, about 8 to 10 minutes.

Divide dough in half. Roll each piece into a 12 x 8-inch rectangle. Place on greased baking sheets. Cover sheets tightly with plastic wrap. Freeze until firm. Transfer to plastic freezer bags. Seal, label, date and return to freezer. Keep frozen up to 4 weeks.

To use: Remove from freezer. Unwrap and place on greased baking sheet. Cover; let stand at room temperature until fully thawed, about 1-1/2 hours. Beginning with an 8-inch end, roll dough as for jelly roll. Pinch seam to seal. With seam side down, press down ends with heel of hand. Fold underneath. Place each roll seam side down, in greased 8 x 4 x 2-inch loaf pan. Cover and let rise in warm place, free from draft, until doubled in bulk, about 1-1/2 hours. Bake at 400° F. for 30 minutes, or until done. Remove from pans and cool on wire rack. Makes 2 loaves.

FREEZER BRIOCHE BRAID

5-1/4 to 6-1/4 cups all purpose flour	1/2 cup milk
1/2 cup sugar	1/2 cup water
1/2 teaspoon salt	2/3 cup margarine
2 packages active dry yeast	4 eggs (at room temperature)
	1 teaspoon lemon extract

In a large bowl thoroughly mix 1 cup flour, 1/2 cup sugar, salt and undissolved yeast. Combine milk, water and margarine in a saucepan. Heat over low heat until liquids are very warm (120° F. to 130° F.). Margarine does not need to melt. Gradually add to dry ingredients and beat 2 minutes at medium speed of electric mixer, scraping bowl occasionally. Add eggs, lemon extract and 1 cup flour. Beat at high speed 2 minutes scraping bowl occasionally. Stir in enough additional flour to make a soft dough. Turn out onto heavily floured board. Knead lightly to form a ball. Cover with a towel; let rest 15 minutes.

Divide dough in half. Divide each half into 3 equal pieces. Form each piece into a roll 12 inches long. Braid 3 rolls together; pinch ends to seal. Repeat with 3 remaining rolls. Place on a large greased baking sheet. Cover tightly with plastic wrap; freeze until firm. Transfer to plastic freezer bags. Seal, label date and return to freezer. Keep frozen up to 4 weeks.

To use: Remove from freezer. Unwrap and place on greased baking sheets. Cover; let stand at room temperature until fully thawed, about 3 hours. Let rise in warm place, free from draft, until doubled in bulk, about 1 hour and 15 minutes.

Combine one egg white with 1 tablespoon sugar; brush mixture on braids. Bake at 350° F. about 25 minutes, or until done. Remove from baking sheets and cool on wire racks. Makes 2 braids.

CINNAMON CRUMB CAKE

5-1/4 to 6-1/4 cups all purpose flour	1/2 cup (1 stick) softened margarine
3/4 cup sugar	1 cup very warm tap water
1 teaspoon salt	(120° F. - 130° F.)
3 packages active dry yeast	3 eggs (at room temperature)
	Melted margarine

Prepare Cinnamon Crumb Topping (below). Refrigerate until ready to use.

In a large bowl thoroughly mix 1-1/4 cups flour, sugar, salt and undissolved yeast. Add softened margarine.

Gradually add tap water to dry ingredients and beat 2 minutes at medium speed of electric mixer, scraping bowl occasionally. Add eggs and 1/4 cup flour. Beat at high speed 2 minutes, scraping bowl occasionally. Stir in enough additional flour to make a soft dough. Turn onto lightly floured board; knead until smooth and elastic, about 8 to 10 minutes.

Divide dough into 4 equal pieces. Roll one piece to fit into a greased 9-inch round or square baking pan. Press dough evenly into pan. Brush with melted margarine. Sprinkle with 1/4 prepared Cinnamon Crumb Topping. Cover pan tightly with plastic wrap, then with aluminum foil. Place in freezer. Repeat with remaining dough and topping. Seal, label and date. Keep frozen up to 4 weeks.

Cinnamon Crumb Topping:

2 cups unsifted flour	4 teaspoons ground cinnamon
1 cup sugar	1 cup (2 sticks) margarine

Blend together flour, sugar, and cinnamon. Mix in margarine just until mixture is crumbly but moist.

To use: Remove from freezer. Let stand, covered with plastic wrap, at room temperature until fully thawed, about 3 hours. Let rise in warm place, free from draft, until doubled in bulk, about 1 hour and 10 minutes. Bake at 375° F. about 20 minutes or until done. Cool in pans on wire racks. Drizzle with confectioners sugar icing (below). Serve hot. Makes 4 9-inch coffee cakes.

Confectioners Sugar Icing:

Sift 2 cups confectioners sugar into a bowl. Gradually add 2 or more tablespoons of hot milk or water until mixture is of a consistency to pour over Crumb Cake.

FREEZER BRAN BREAD

9 to 10 cups all purpose flour
3 cups whole bran cereal
   with wheat germ
1/4 cup sugar
4 teaspoons salt
3 packages active dry yeast

1/2 cup (1 stick)
   softened margarine
3 cups very warm tap water
   (120° F. - 130° F.)
1/3 cup dark molasses
   (at room temperature)
Melted margarine

In a large bowl thoroughly mix 2 cups flour, cereal, sugar, salt and undissolved yeast. Add softened margarine. Gradually add very warm tap water and molasses to dry ingredients and beat 2 minutes at medium speed of electric mixer, scraping bowl occasionally. Add 1 cup flour. Beat at high speed 2 minutes, scraping bowl occasionally. Stir in enough additional flour to make a stiff dough. Turn onto lightly floured board; knead until smooth and elastic, about 12 minutes. Cover, let rise on board 15 minutes. Roll dough out to an 18 x 12-inch rectangle. Cut into 3 equal pieces, 6 x 12-inches each. Brush with melted margarine. Stack dough on a greased baking sheet, brushed side up, placing plastic wrap between each piece. Cover sheet tightly with plastic wrap. Place in freezer. When frozen, separate pieces of dough and wrap with freezer wrap or freezer plastic bags. Seal, label, date. Keep frozen up to 4 weeks.

To use: Remove from freezer. Unwrap and place on ungreased baking sheet, brushed side up. Cover; let stand at room temperature until fully thawed, about 2-1/2 hours. Knead each piece of dough to form a ball, then press into a 6-inch mound. Place each on greased baking sheet. Cover; let rise in warm place, free from draft, until doubled in bulk, about 2-1/2 hours.

Bake at 350° F. 40 to 45 minutes or until done. Remove from baking sheets and cool on wire racks. Makes 3 round loaves.

ORANGE DATE NUT LOAF

4 cups all purpose flour	2 teaspoons grated orange rind
1 teaspoon salt	1/4 cup lemon juice
4 teaspoons baking powder	1-1/2 cups milk
1 cup butter or margarine	1 cup chopped walnuts
2 cups sugar	1 cup sugar-rolled chopped dates
4 eggs, beaten	

Mix flour with salt and baking powder. Cream butter. Gradually add sugar and beat until light and fluffy. Add eggs and orange rind and beat until smooth. Add flour mixture alternately with lemon juice and milk. Fold in nuts and dates. Spoon into 2 greased and floured 9 x 5-inch loaf pans. Bake at 350° F. for 1 hour or until toothpick inserted in center of top comes out clean. Cool on rack in pan 10 minutes. Remove from pan. Cool loaf on rack. Wrap cooled bread in freezer wrap. Seal, label, date and freeze.

To use: Remove bread from freezer and let defrost at room temperature. Bread will slice more easily while still slightly frozen.

POTATO ROLLS

1 package active dry yeast	1 cup softened butter
1 cup lukewarm water	or margarine
1 cup unseasoned mashed potato	2 teaspoons salt
1 cup sugar	6 cups (approximate)
4 eggs, beaten	all purpose flour

Dissolve yeast in water. Add mashed potatoes and sugar. Cover lightly and let stand overnight in a warm place.

Next day add eggs, butter and salt. Stir in half the flour and beat well. Gradually stir in remaining flour until dough is stiff enough to roll out on a floured board. Roll 1/2-inch thick and cut 2-inch rounds. Place the rounds 1-inch apart on a greased baking sheet. Cover and let rise in a warm place until doubled in bulk. Bake at 400° F. 10 minutes. Makes 4 dozen. Cool rolls on a rack, put into freezer bags. Seal, label, date, freeze.

To use: Remove as many as needed from freezer. Wrap in aluminum foil and heat at 400° F. about 10 minutes.

ANADAMA BREAD

7 to 8 cups all purpose flour
1-1/4 cups yellow cornmeal
2-1/2 teaspoons salt
2 packages active dry yeast

1/3 cup softened butter
  or margarine
2-1/4 cups very warm tap water
  (120° F. - 130° F.)
2/3 cup molasses
  (at room temperature)

In a large bowl thoroughly mix 2-1/2 cups flour, cornmeal, salt and yeast. Add butter or margarine. Gradually add tap water and molasses to dry ingredients and beat two minutes at medium speed of electric mixer, scraping bowl occasionally. Add 1/2 cup flour. Beat at high speed two minutes, scraping bowl occasionally. Stir in enough additional flour to make a stiff dough. Turn out onto lightly floured board and knead until smooth and elastic, about 8 to 10 minutes. Place in greased bowl, turning to grease top. Cover and let rise in a warm place, free from draft, until doubled in bulk, about one hour. Punch dough down. Divide in half. Roll each half to a 14 x 9-inch rectangle. Shape into rolls by rolling up dough, jelly roll style, starting at shorter end. Place in two greased 9 x 5 x 3-inch loaf pans. Cover, let rise in warm place, free from draft, until doubled in bulk, about 45 minutes. Bake at 375° F. about 45 minutes or until done. Remove from pan and cool on racks. Wrap cooled bread in freezer wrap. Seal, label date and free.

To use: Let frozen bread defrost to room temperature, about 2 hours.

MUFFINS

---

6 tablespoons shortening

6 tablespoons sugar

2 eggs, beaten

4 cups all purpose flour

6 teaspoons baking powder

2 teaspoons salt

2 cups milk

Grease well and flour 24 2-inch muffin pans.

Cream shortening with sugar until light. Add eggs and beat well. Mix flour with baking powder and salt. Add alternately with milk to shortening mixture, stirring just to blend.

Fill muffin pans 2/3 full. Bake at 400° F. for 20-25 minutes. Remove from pans and cool on rack.

To freeze: Pack muffins in family size units in plastic freezer bags. Seal, label and date. Makes 2 dozen.

Storage time: Up to 6 months.

To use: Remove from freezer and defrost or wrap in aluminum foil and heat at 400° F. for 10 minutes.

BANANA BREAD

---

4 cups all purpose flour

1 teaspoon baking powder

1 teaspoon baking soda

1 teaspoon salt

1/2 cup butter or margarine

1/2 cup sugar

2 eggs, well beaten

1-1/3 cups mashed banana

6 tablespoons buttermilk

Grease and flour well 2 4 x 8-inch loaf pans.

Mix flour with baking powder, soda and salt. Cream butter and sugar until light and fluffy. Beat in eggs. Fold in mashed banana. Add flour mixture alternately with buttermilk to creamed mixture stirring just to blend. Spoon into 2 loaf pans. Bake at 350° F. 50-60 minutes or until a toothpick inserted in center comes out clean. Cool in pans 10 minutes on rack. Carefully remove loaves from pans and cool on rack. When cool, wrap in freezer wrap and label, date, seal and freeze.

To use: Unwrap loosely and defrost. (Bread cuts more easily while still slightly frozen).

Storage time: Up to 3 months.

NUT BREAD

6 cups all purpose flour	2 cups milk
3 tablespoons baking powder	2 cups chopped walnuts
2 teaspoons salt	or pecans
1 cup sugar	1/2 cup melted butter
4 eggs, well beaten	or margarine

Grease well and flour 2 9x5-inch loaf pans.

Mix flour, baking powder, salt and sugar in a bowl. Combine eggs and milk. Stir into flour mixture just to blend. Stir in nuts and cooled melted butter. Spoon into 2 loaf pans. Bake at 350° F. 50-60 minutes or until a toothpick inserted in center comes out clean. Cool in pans 10 minutes on rack. Carefully remove loaves from pans and cool on rack. When cool, wrap in freezer wrap and label, date, seal and freeze.

To use: Unwrap loosely and defrost. (Bread cuts more easily while still slightly frozen).

Storage time: Up to 3 months.

Cakes and Cookies

CAKES AND COOKIES

It is comforting to know there is a cake in the freezer for unexpected company, a celebration, or any occasion. Baked cakes freeze very well, cake dough less well. Cookies freeze well both when baked or as raw dough.

How to's With Cake

- Freeze frosted cakes before wrapping to avoid messing the frosting.
- Cut "ice box" cookies while still frozen and bake at once.
- Let drop cookie batter warm up a bit before baking.
- Wrap cake layers in freezer wrap, freeze — store in freezer in cardboard boxes to avoid crushing. Freeze and store baked cookies the same way.
- Use pure vanilla extract for flavoring cakes to be frozen. Synthetic vanilla may become bitter during storage.
- Be sure to put baking directions on label of unbaked frozen cookie dough.

Storage Time for Cakes and Cookies

Cakes, plain or frosted .... 4 to 6 months
Cookies, baked .... 4 to 6 months
Cookie dough .... 4 months

MINCEMEAT COFFEE CAKE

2 cups all purpose flour
3/4 cup sugar
2-1/2 teaspoons baking powder
1/2 teaspoon salt
1/2 cup shortening

1 egg
1/2 cup milk
3/4 cup moist mincemeat
1/2 cup nuts

Mix flour with sugar, baking powder and salt in bowl. Cut in shortening with 2 knives or pastry blender. Beat egg with milk and add with mincemeat and nuts to flour mixture, stirring enough to blend. Spoon batter into greased and floured 8x8x2-inch square pan. Bake at 375° F. 35-40 minutes. Cool on rack. Remove cake from pan. Wrap with freezer wrap. Seal, label, date, freeze.

To use: Wrap cake in aluminum foil and heat at 375° F. 10-15 minutes. Serve hot in squares.

CARROT CAKE

3 cups all purpose flour
2 teaspoons baking powder
2 teaspoons baking soda
1-1/2 teaspoons cinnamon
1/2 teaspoon salt

2 cups sugar
1-1/2 cups corn oil
4 eggs
2 cups finely grated carrots
1/2 cup chopped pecans

Mix flour, baking powder, soda, cinnamon, salt and sugar in large bowl of mixer. Add oil gradually, beating on low speed. Add eggs, one at a time, beating into batter. Stir in carrots and pecans. Spoon into a greased and floured 10 cup Bundt pan and bake at 375° F. for 1 hour and 10 minutes or until toothpick inserted in top comes out clean. Cool on rack for 10 minutes. Remove cake from pan and cool on rack. Wrap in freezer wrap. Seal, label, date, freeze.

To use: Defrost cake at room temperature. Serve plain or frost with confectioners sugar icing.

Note: Baked cake may be cut into halves or quarters, wrapped and frozen, if it is more convenient to use a smaller portion at one time.

ORANGE ALMOND COOKIES

1 cup shortening
1/2 cup butter or
    margarine
3/4 cup granulated sugar
3/4 cup light brown sugar,
    firmly packed
3 eggs

1-1/2 tablespoons
    grated orange rind
4 cups all purpose flour
3/4 teaspoon soda
1 teaspoon salt
3/4 cup chopped,
    blanched almonds

Cream shortening and butter until soft. Gradually beat in sugar until light and creamy. Add eggs and grated orange rind and beat well. Mix flour with soda and salt and add to creamed mixture with almonds. Chill dough and shape into 2 rolls 9 to 10-inches long and 2-inches square. Wrap in freezer wrap. Seal, label, date, freeze. Makes 9 dozen cookies.

To use: Cut rolls into thin slices and bake at 400° F. 6 to 8 minutes.

APPLESAUCE OATMEAL COOKIES

1 cup all purpose flour
2 cups quick cooking oatmeal
1/2 teaspoon cinnamon
1/2 teaspoon nutmeg
1/4 teaspoon salt
1 cup chopped raisins
1 cup chopped nuts

1/2 cup shortening
1 cup sugar
1 cup frozen applesauce,
    defrosted
1 teaspoon soda
1 egg, well beaten

Mix flour with oatmeal, spices, salt, raisins and nuts. Cream shortening and sugar until light and fluffy. Mix applesauce with soda. Add with egg to creamed mixture and fold in dry ingredients. Pack into freezer containers. Leave head space. Seal, label, date, freeze.

To use: Partially defrost batter. Drop by teaspoonsful on a greased cookie sheet. Bake at 375° F. for about 15 minutes or until lightly browned. Makes 6 dozen cookies.

HONEY FRUIT CAKE

2/3 cup shortening
1-1/2 cups honey
1/2 teaspoon salt
3 eggs
3 cups all purpose flour
3 teaspoons baking powder

1 teaspoon cinnamon
1 teaspoon cloves
1/2 cup orange juice
2 cups chopped raisins
1 cup chopped almonds

Grease and line with parchment paper 2 4x8-inch loaf pans.

Beat together shortening, honey, salt and eggs. Mix flour with baking powder and spices. Add alternately with fruit juice to honey mixture, mixing well after each addition. Fold in raisins and almonds.

Spoon into loaf pans and bake at 325° F. for 1 hour or until a toothpick inserted in center comes out clean. Cool on rack in pans for 10 minutes. Carefully remove from pans, peel off paper and cool on rack. Wrap loaves in freezer wrap. Seal, label, date and freeze.

Storage time: 3 months.

To use: Unwrap loosely and defrost. (Cake cuts more easily when slightly frozen.)

GINGER SLICES

4 cups all purpose flour
1 teaspoon baking soda
1 tablespoon powdered ginger
1/4 teaspoon salt

1 cup butter or margarine
1/2 cup dark brown sugar,
    firmly packed
3/4 cup molasses
2 eggs

Mix flour, soda, ginger and salt.

Cream butter with brown sugar until light and fluffy. Beat in the molasses and eggs. Fold in flour mixture, beating well. Chill dough and then shape into two rolls, 2-inches in diameter. Wrap in freezer wrap, seal, label, date and freeze.

Storage time: 1 to 2 months.

To use: Cut frozen cookie bars into thin slices. Place on greased cookie sheets. Bake at 350° F. 10-12 minutes or until lightly browned. Whole recipe makes 6 dozen.

GRAHAM CRACKER TORTE CAKE

1/4 cup butter or margarine
1 cup sugar
3 egg yolks
1 teaspoon vanilla
1 cup chopped pecans

2-1/4 cups fine graham
    cracker crumbs
2 teaspoons baking powder
1/2 teaspoon salt
3/4 cup milk
1 egg white stiffly beaten

Cream butter and sugar until fluffy. Beat in egg yolks and vanilla, beating well. Fold in nuts. Mix crumbs with baking powder and salt. Add alternately with milk in 3 additions, beating well after each addition. Fold in beaten egg white.

Spoon batter into 2 greased and floured 9-inch layer cake pans. Bake at 350° F. about 30 minutes or until top springs back when touched with the finger. Cool on rack in pans 5 minutes. Carefully remove from pans and cool cake on rack. When cooled, wrap in freezer wrap. Seal, label, date and freeze.

Storage time: Up to 2 months.

To serve: Unwrap loosely and defrost layers. Place one layer on cake plate. Spread with 1/2 to 3/4 cup strawberry jam. Place second layer on top of jam and top cake with sweetened whipped cream. Keep chilled until ready to serve. Makes 8-10 servings.

LEMONY SQUARES

1/2 cup butter
1 cup sugar
2 eggs
1-1/2 cups all purpose flour
1-1/2 teaspoons baking powder

1/4 teaspoon salt
1/2 cup milk
1 teaspoon grated lemon rind
2/3 cup sugar
1/4 cup lemon juice

Cream butter and 1 cup sugar until light and fluffy. Beat in eggs, flour, baking powder and salt. Add milk to creamed mixture. Stir in grated lemon rind. Spoon batter into greased and floured 13 x 9-inch pan. Bake at 350° F. for 25 minutes or until top springs back when touched with finger. Mix 2/3 cup sugar with lemon juice and spoon over cake. Bake 5 minutes longer. Cut into squares when still warm. Cool. Freeze squares. Wrap in freezer wrap in family size portions. Seal, label, date and return to freezer. Squares can be stored in boxes to avoid damage. Makes 28 squares.

Storage time: Up to 3 months.
To use: Defrost.

NUTSIES

2-1/2 cups whole wheat flour
2 teaspoons baking powder
1/4 teaspoon salt
1 cup chopped almonds
1/2 cup shortening

1-1/3 cups sugar
2 teaspoons vanilla extract
4 teaspoons grated orange rind
2 eggs
1/4 cup milk

Mix flour, baking powder and salt. Stir in nuts.

Cream shortening and sugar until light and fluffy. Beat in vanilla, orange rind and eggs. Add flour mixture alternately with milk, stirring just to blend. Spread in a greased and floured 15 x 10-inch shallow pan. Bake at 350° F. for 18-20 minutes. While still warm, cut in squares. Cool. To freeze: pack into family size portions and wrap in freezer wrap. Seal, label, date and freeze.

To use: Defrost. Recipe makes 60 squares.
Storage time: 2 months.

PEANUT BUTTER COOKIES

1 cup butter or margarine
1 cup granulated sugar
1 cup light brown sugar,
    firmly packed
1 cup peanut butter

1 teaspoon salt
2 eggs slightly beaten
1 teaspoon vanilla extract
2-1/2 cups all purpose flour
1 teaspoon baking soda

Cream together butter, sugars and peanut butter until light and fluffy. Beat in salt, eggs and vanilla. Mix flour with soda and fold into creamed mixture. Pack into several freezer containers. Seal, label, date and freeze.

Storage time: Up to 2 months.

To use: Defrost batter. Shape into 1-inch balls. Place on greased baking sheet. Push down with fork tines to form a criss-cross pattern. Bake at 350° F. 10 minutes or until lightly browned. Whole recipe makes 5 dozen.

Casseroles and Soups

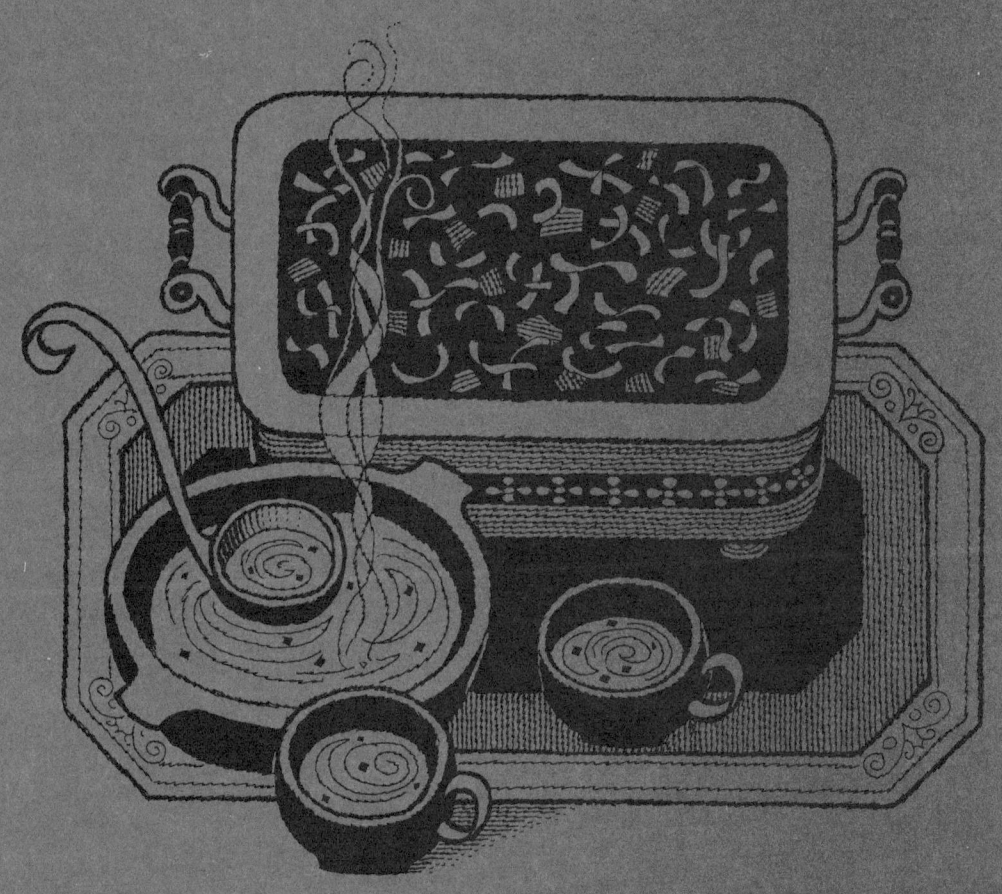

CASSEROLES AND SOUPS

One good way to take advantage of the convenience of a freezer is to use it for freezing casserole main dishes. Whether they are prepared already cooked or ready to cook, they will be a big help when you are pressed for time.

How to's With Casseroles

- Use your own favorite recipes. Undercook, since foods tend to become overcooked when being reheated.
- Season lightly. Pepper and cloves tend to become bitter when frozen. Foods can be seasoned when heated.
- For meat and poultry pies the unbaked crust can be added before freezing or at time of baking.
- Line greased casserole with heavy duty aluminum foil. Bring it up over side of dish enough to cover top. Fill foil lined dish with food. Bake, if desired, or freeze unbaked. Cover top of dish with extra foil. When frozen solid remove food from dish. Seal, label, date. Overwrap with plastic wrap if desired. When ready to use remove wrapping, place in same casserole and heat.
- Freeze meat loaf baked. It has better quality, than when frozen unbaked.
- Cooked turkey or chicken in casseroles freezes well.
- Add buttered crumbs when casserole is being heated.
- When preparing a favorite dish make twice the recipe at one time and freeze one-half.
- Cooked dry beans freeze well. Undercook as they soften during freezing.
- Always leave head space when freezing main dishes in containers. Leave 1/2-inch for pints, 1-inch for quarts.
- When freezing main dishes pour 1/3 in container, add a layer of plastic wrap or foil, pour in another third, add another layer of plastic wrap or foil and fill container, leaving head space. Seal, label, date, freeze. This layering allows blocks of frozen food to be separated when defrosting, and hastens heating.
- Cool food to be frozen quickly by immersing pan in cold or ice water.
- To reheat frozen foods unwrap and place in pan or casserole in which it was frozen. Preheat oven to temperature required in recipe and heat in oven until food is hot and bubbly. Allow at least one hour depending on amount of food and temperature.
- Or food can be defrosted and heated in top of double boiler or in saucepan over very low heat.
- Food thickened with cornstarch or flour may seem to separate on defrosting, but it will become smooth when heated.

Storage Time for Casseroles

Most combination dishes can be stored up to 6 months.

LASAGNA TO FREEZE

2-1/4 pounds ground beef
2/3 cup chopped onion
2 cloves garlic, crushed
4 teaspoons salt
1/2 teaspoon Tabasco sauce
1 tablespoon oregano
3 tablespoons dried parsley
3 cans (6-ounce) tomato paste
3 cans (8-ounce) tomato sauce

2-1/4 cups hot water
3 eggs, beaten
3 pounds cream style
   cottage cheese
18 lasagna noodles, cooked
   (about 1 pound, uncooked)
3/4 pound Process
   Cheddar cheese, grated
3/4 cup grated Parmesan cheese

Line four 8-inch square baking pans with aluminum foil, allowing enough to come over top.

Cook ground beef until lightly browned. Add onion and garlic and cook until tender. Drain off fat. Add seasonings, tomato paste, tomato sauce and water. Cook and stir 5 minutes.

Blend eggs with cottage cheese.

In each pan spread a layer of meat mixture. (About 3/4 cup per pan). Add a layer of noodles, a layer of meat, a layer of cottage cheese mixture, process cheese and Parmesan cheese. Repeat layers until all ingredients are used. Fold wrapping around top of pan. Seal, label, date, freeze at once. When frozen remove from pan and overwrap with plastic wrap, if desired.

To use: Remove wrappings. Place in greased baking pan. (Use the same one in which it was frozen). Bake at 400° F. for 1-1/4 hours or until sauce bubbles at edges and center is hot. Each pan makes 6 servings.

CHICKEN TAMBOURI

2 pounds green or
    yellow split peas
2-1/4 quarts boiling water
2 garlic cloves, crushed
3 teaspoons salt
1/4 cup butter or
    margarine
1-1/2 cups chopped onion

12 to 16 chicken pieces
1/4 cup corn oil
1 teaspoon dried leaf thyme
1/2 teaspoon dried rosemary
2 cans (10-1/2 ounce) condensed
    cream of mushroom soup
1-1/3 cups milk

Line two 1-1/2-2 quart casseroles with aluminum foil, allowing enough to come over top.

Pick over and wash split peas. Add to boiling water. Bring to boiling point and boil 2 minutes. Remove from heat, stir in crushed garlic and salt. Let stand, covered 1/2 hour.

Cook onion in butter, over low heat until soft. Remove from skillet. Reserve. Add oil and brown chicken on all sides.

Spoon split peas into two casseroles. Spread onions over peas. Put chicken pieces into peas, pushing down to partly cover chicken. Mix herbs and sprinkle over chicken. Combine mushroom soup with milk in skillet in which chicken was fried. Heat and pour over chicken and peas. Cool. Fold wrapping around top of casserole and seal. Label, date and freeze at once. When frozen, remove from casserole dish and overwrap with plastic wrap, if desired.

To use: Remove wrappings. Place in greased casserole (use the same one in which it was frozen). Bake at 350° F. for 1 hour 45 minutes. Cover lightly with foil while baking. Each casserole makes 6 to 8 servings.

EGGPLANT ACADIAN

2 cups frozen diced eggplant
2 tablespoons butter
    or margarine
3/4 cup frozen, diced onion
3/4 cup frozen
    diced green pepper
2 cups defrosted, frozen, stewed
    tomatoes, strained

3 tablespoons flour
1/2 teaspoon salt
1 tablespoon brown sugar
1/4 bay leaf, cut up
1/8 teaspoon ground cloves
2 tablespoons grated
    Parmesan cheese
1/3 cup fine, dry bread crumbs

Butter a 6-cup casserole and put eggplant in dish.

Heat butter and saute onion and green pepper until tender but not browned. Stir in flour. Add tomatoes and seasonings. Cook and stir 5 minutes. Pour over eggplant. Mix cheese and crumbs and sprinkle over casserole. Bake at 350° F. for 30 minutes or until hot and bubbly. Makes 6 servings.

DOWN SOUTH CASSEROLE

2 cups diced, cooked ham
1 tablespoon butter or
    margarine
4 cups frozen mashed
    sweet potatoes, defrosted
2 tablespoons brown sugar

1 egg, well beaten
1/2 cup hot milk
1/2 teaspoon salt
1/8 teaspoon nutmeg
1/8 teaspoon allspice

Brown ham quickly in butter. Mix sweet potatoes with remaining ingredients, beat well. Fold in ham. Spoon into a buttered 2-quart casserole. Bake at 350° F. for 30 minutes or until nicely browned. Makes 4 to 6 servings.

STUFFED TOMATO CASSEROLE

9 ripe tomatoes	3 cups soft fresh bread crumbs
2 tablespoons minced onion	1 teaspoon salt
2 tablespoons minced parsley	1/2 teaspoon marjoram
1/4 cup butter or margarine	1 teaspoon basil

Dip tomatoes in boiling water for 30 seconds then in cold water. Remove skin. Cut out stem end. With a spoon, remove inside of tomato to make a shell and chop pulp. Combine with onion, parsley and butter and mix well. Mix into bread crumbs, salt, marjoram and basil. Fill into tomato shells. Place in aluminum foil baking dish. Cover. Seal, label, date and freeze.

Storage time: Up to 3 months.

To use: Place number of tomatoes needed in buttered baking dish. Defrost and bake at 400° F. for 20 minutes.

SWEET POTATOES WITH FRUIT

8 cooked medium sweet potatoes	1/3 cup brown sugar,
1-1/2 cups chopped cranberries	firmly packed
1-1/2 cups finely diced apples	1-1/2 teaspoons salt
	1/3 cup butter or margarine

Grease and line 2 6-cup casseroles with aluminum foil, leaving enough to cover top. Peel sweet potatoes and slice a layer into casseroles. Mix cranberries, apples, brown sugar and salt and layer over potatoes. Continue until fruit and potatoes are used. Dot top of each casserole with butter. Freeze. When frozen, bring aluminum foil around top of food, seal, label, date and return to freezer.

Storage time: Up to 3 months.

To use: Remove foil and place food in greased casserole in which potatoes were originally frozen. Defrost. Bake at 350° F. 35-40 minutes or until browned and bubbly. Makes 4 to 6 servings.

TURKEY HASH

1 cup diced onion
1 cup diced celery
1/4 cup butter or
   margarine
2 cups turkey or chicken
   broth

4 cups light and dark meat
   of cooked turkey, finely cut
2 teaspoons cornstarch
1/4 cup dry white wine

Saute onion and celery in margarine until tender but not browned. Add turkey meat and turkey broth and mix lightly to blend. Mix cornstarch with wine and add to turkey mixture. Cook and stir over low heat until mixture is thickened. Cool at once. Spoon into 2-3 cup containers. Leave head space. Seal, label, date, freeze.

To use: Defrost 1 container in top of double boiler or heat over very low heat. Add salt and pepper to taste and 2 teaspoons butter. Serve over thin slices of toasted corn bread. Each container makes 4 servings.

SOUPS

Soups are another good food to freeze. Homemade soups or broths are marvelous for winter lunches, suppers or to serve in cups after an evening of sports. Since most soups are long cooking, make a large "batch" and freeze in several containers.

How to's With Soup

- Keep a container with a snap-on lid in the freezer and add vegetable cooking liquids to it as they accumulate. This includes potato, green bean, carrots, peas. Have a separate container marked for strong vegetable liquids such as cabbage and broccoli. Use instead of water when making broth from bones.
- Concentrate broths before freezing. They take less freezer space and water can be added when defrosted.
- Be sure to allow head space in container when freezing soups.
- Save bones trimmed from meats, ham bones, chicken and turkey carcasses and trimmings. Freeze and use for making broths and soups as needed.

Storage Time for Soups

Most soups and broths will store well up to 3 months.

Recipes to freeze

ZUCCHINI SOUP

8 slices bacon, cut up	5 cups water
2 cups chopped onion	2 teaspoons salt
12 medium zucchini squash	2 teaspoons dried basil leaves
2-1/2 cups beef broth	1/2 cup chopped parsley

In a large saucepan, brown bacon, stirring. Pour off all but 2 tablespoons fat. Add onion, cook and stir until tender. Wash and trim zucchini and chop finely. Add with remaining ingredients to bacon and onion. Bring to a boil. Simmer, uncovered, 15 minutes. Cool at once. Spoon into four 1-quart containers, leaving head space. Seal, label, date, freeze.

To use: Defrost soup and heat to boiling. Add pepper to taste. Serve with grated Parmesan cheese. Each container makes 4 1-cup servings.

BLACK BEAN SOUP

2 cups dried black beans
2 onions, sliced
1 cup chopped celery
2 quarts water

6 tablespoons butter or
 margarine
1/4 teaspoon dry mustard
2 teaspoons salt

Pick over and wash beans. Soak overnight in water to cover. Saute onion and celery in butter in a 4 quart saucepan. Add drained beans, 2 quarts water, mustard and salt. Bring to a boil and simmer covered, about 3 hours or until tender. If bean mixture seems too thick add more water. Puree in small amount at a time in the blender. Taste and correct seasonings. Chill. Put into 3 1-quart containers. Seal, label, date and freeze.

Storage time: Up to 3 months.

To use: Defrost container of soup and heat. Add 4 tablespoons sherry. Serve with a thin slice of lemon in each dish. Each container makes 4 servings.

CREAM OF MUSHROOM SOUP

1/2 pound fresh mushrooms,
 chopped
1/4 cup butter or margarine
2 tablespoons flour

1 cup chicken stock
1 quart milk
1 cup cream
1 teaspoon salt

Saute mushrooms in butter for 5 minutes uncovered. Cover and cook 5 minutes more. Blend in flour. Add chicken stock, milk and cream gradually and cook and stir until thickened. Season with salt. Chill. Pour into 2 1-quart containers. Seal, label, date, and freeze.

Storage time: 3 months.

To serve: Defrost container and heat. If separation occurs stir with a whisk. Add freshly ground pepper and grated nutmeg to taste. Each container makes 4 servings.

CREAM OF ASPARAGUS SOUP

2 cups fresh asparagus
4 cups water or
   vegetable liquid
2 cups chicken broth
1/4 cup chopped onion
1/2 cup minced celery

3 tablespoons butter
   or margarine
3 tablespoons flour
Salt and freshly ground
   pepper to taste

Snap off tough ends of asparagus and discard. Wash remaining asparagus well, remove scales and wash again. Cut into 1-inch pieces and cook in water with onion and celery until tender. Puree a small amount at a time in the blender and add to chicken broth. Cream butter and flour together and blend into hot liquid with a whisk and bring to a boil. Season to taste with salt and pepper. Chill. Pour into 2 1-quart containers. Seal, label, date and freeze.

Storage time: 3 months.

To serve: Defrost container of soup and heat. Blend in 1/2 cup cream and season with grated nutmeg. Each containers makes 4 servings.

LEEK AND POTATO SOUP

6 leeks
1/4 cup butter or
 margarine
1 large onion, sliced
3 cups beef broth
 or vegetable liquid

3 cups water
1/2 teaspoon dried thyme
1 bay leaf
2 cups diced raw potato

Clean leeks and wash well. Remove stem ends and cut into thin slices. Saute in butter with onion slices until soft. Add remaining ingredients and simmer about 20 minutes. Remove bay leaf and cool at once. Spoon into three 1-quart containers. Leave head space. Seal, label, date, freeze.

To use: Defrost 1 container. Add salt and pepper to taste and 1/2 cup rich milk, heat to boiling. Each container makes 4 servings.

BEAN 'N HAM SOUP

2 pounds dried pea beans
4 quarts cold water
1 ham bone

4 medium onions
6 carrots
Salt to taste

Pick over and wash beans. Soak overnight in 2 quarts water. Next morning, in a large kettle, add remaining 2 quarts water, bring to a boil and add ham bone. Simmer about 1 hour or until beans are almost tender. Remove ham bone and cool.

Peel and chop onions and carrots. Clean and dice celery. Add to beans and simmer 15 minutes longer. Dice any meat from ham bone and return to soup. Cool at once and spoon into six quart containers. Leave head space. Seal, label, date, freeze.

To use: Defrost one container. Add 1 cup water and heat to boiling. Season to taste with pepper and sprinkle each serving with chopped celery. Each container makes 4 servings.

Desserts

DESSERTS

With a freezer you can have desserts ready for your family or special occasions. You can make your own ice cream to store or a favorite pie.

How to's With Desserts

- The preferred method for freezing fruit pies is unbaked.
- Add extra gelatin to gelatin desserts to freeze since freezing has a tendency to cause separation.
- Pie or desserts with whipped cream or whipped topping used as a decoration should be first frozen, then wrapped.
- Package wrapped frozen products in boxes to keep from being damaged in freezer.
- Roll and cut pastry in a size to fit pie shell. Place on large cardboard circle covered with plastic wrap, separate pastry circles with plastic wrap. Overwrap with freezer wrap, seal, label, date, freeze. To use, defrost slightly and fit into pie plate.
- Prepare for holidays in advance. Make favorite steamed pudding, cool. Package in mold and seal with freezer tape or wrap in freezer wrap, seal, label, date, freeze. When ready to use, remove wrapping and place frozen pudding in steamer or top of double boiler. Heat to serving temperature.

Recipes to freeze

FRESH PEACH PIE

Pastry: Mix 2 cups sifted all purpose flour with 1 teaspoon salt in a bowl. Add 1/2 cup corn oil and mix thoroughly with a fork. Sprinkle 2 tablespoons cold water over flour—oil mixture and mix well. Divide dough into almost half. Flatten larger portion slightly and roll out into 12-inch circle between 2 pieces of wax paper. Peel off paper and fit pastry into a 9-inch pie plate. Trim dough 1/2-inch beyond edge, if necessary. Roll out remaining in circle.

Filling:

2/3 cup sugar	5 cups sliced fresh peaches
2 tablespoons cornstarch	1/4 teaspoon crystalline
1/8 teaspoon salt	ascorbic acid
	1 tablespoon margarine

Mix sugar, cornstarch and salt. Mix peaches with ascorbic acid dissolved in 2 tablespoons water. Put 1/2 sugar mixture in bottom of pie shell. Add peaches, top with remaining sugar and margarine. Cover with pastry and flute edges to seal. Wrap with freezer wrap. Seal, label, date, freeze.

To use: Remove wrappings. Cut vent holes in upper crust. Bake at 450° F. 15 to 20 minutes. Reduce heat to 375° F. and bake 35-40 minutes longer.

PECAN PIE

3 eggs
1 cup dark corn syrup
1 cup sugar
2 tablespoons melted margarine

1 teaspoon vanilla extract
1/8 teaspoon salt
1 cup pecans, halved or chopped
1 unbaked 9-inch pastry shell

Mix together eggs, corn syrup, sugar, margarine, vanilla, salt and pecans. Pour into pastry shell. Bake at 400° F. for 15 minutes. Reduce heat to 350° F. and bake 30 to 35 minutes longer. Outer edge of filling should be set, center slightly soft. Cool. Wrap pie in freezer wrap. Seal, label, date, freeze.

To use: Remove wrapping. Heat frozen pie at 350° F. 30-35 minutes. Makes 8 to 10 servings.

FROZEN COFFEE PIE

1 baked 8-inch pastry shell
1/2 cup dark corn syrup
2 egg yolks

1 tablespoon freeze dried coffee
1 teaspoon vanilla extract
1 cup heavy cream, whipped

Mix together in small heavy saucepan, dark corn syrup, egg yolks and salt. Cook over low heat, stirring constantly, until mixture just reaches boiling point. Add coffee, continue stirring constantly, until coffee completely dissolves. Remove from heat, stir in vanilla; cool at room temperature. Gradually fold egg mixture into whipped cream until blended. Turn cream mixture into pie shell, place in freezer until cream mixture is firm. Wrap in freezer wrap, seal, label, date.

To use: Remove from freezer 20 minutes before serving. Garnish with 2 tablespoons chopped pistachio nuts. Makes 6 servings.

CRANBERRY PIE

Pastry for 1 8-inch pie
2 cups raw cranberries
1 cup sugar

1/2 cup water
1-1/2 tablespoons cornstarch
1 tablespoon butter
or margarine

Line 8-inch pie plate with pastry and flute edge. Wash cranberries and mix with sugar and water. Bring to a boil and cook 5 minutes. Add cornstarch to 2 tablespoons water and quickly stir into cranberries. Add butter and cook until thickened. Chill. Spoon into pie shell. Freeze. Wrap in freezer wrap. Seal, label, date and return to freezer.

Storage time: 2 months.

To use: Defrost and bake at 350° F. 25-35 minutes. Place marshmallows on top to completely cover and bake 5 minutes more or until marshmallows are browned. Serve warm.

CHOCOLATE CHIFFON PIE

1-1/2 tablespoons
    unflavored gelatin
3 tablespoons cold water
2 squares (2-ounces)
    unsweetened chocolate
1/2 cup boiling water

4 eggs, separated
3/4 cup sugar
1 teaspoon vanilla extract
1/2 cup heavy cream, whipped
1 9-inch baked pie shell

Soften gelatin in cold water. Melt chocolate in top of double boiler. Gradually add boiling water, stirring to blend. Add gelatin and stir until dissolved. Remove from heat. Beat egg yolks until creamy with 1/2 cup of the sugar and beat into the gelatin mixture. Refrigerate until mixture begins to thicken. Add vanilla.

Whip egg whites with remaining sugar until stiff and fold into chocolate mixture. Spoon into baked pie shell. Chill until firm. Spread with whipped cream. Freeze. Wrap in freezer wrap. Seal, label, date and return to freezer.

Storage time: 2 months.

To use: Defrost or can be served partially frozen. Makes 1 pie.

CHOCOLATE MOUSSE

1 cup milk
3/4 cup sugar
1 teaspoon unflavored gelatin

2 squares (2 ounces)
    unsweetened chocolate
1 teaspoon vanilla extract
2 cups heavy cream, whipped

Scald milk with sugar, gelatin and chocolate, stirring constantly with whisk to blend smoothly. Let cool, add vanilla. Freeze in freezer in flat pan until mushy. Put into chilled bowl and whip until light. Fold in whipped cream. Spoon into a 6-cup mold, preferably metal. Cover, label, date and freeze.

Storage time: 1 month.

To serve: When ready to serve, dip mold quickly in warm water and invert mold on a chilled platter. Let soften in refrigerator 20-30 minutes. Slice and serve. Makes 6 servings.

INDIVIDUAL BAKED ALASKA

6 egg whites
Dash salt
3/4 cup sugar

8 slices pound cake,
    about 1/2-inch thick
1 quart brick ice cream,
    any flavor

Beat egg whites with salt until foamy. Gradually beat in sugar, beating until stiff peaks are formed. Place cake on pan. Cut brick ice cream in slices slightly smaller than cake. Cover cake and ice cream with meringue, working quickly. Put in freezer and freeze until firm. Place in a box, seal, label, date and return to freezer.

Storage time: 3 months.

To use: Place on baking pan covered with brown paper. Brown at 450° F. for 5 minutes. Makes 8 servings.

FROZEN SUMMER REFRESHER

1 envelope unflavored gelatin
3 cups water
1/2 cup sugar
1-1/3 cups instant
    nonfat dry milk

1/2 cup corn oil
1/3 cup light corn syrup
2/3 crushed hard peppermint candy
1 teaspoon vanilla extract
1/2 teaspoon salt

In small saucepan sprinkle gelatin over 1 cup of the water to soften. Stir in sugar. Heat over medium heat, stirring constantly, just until dissolved. (Do not boil). Remove from heat. In large bowl, sprinkle dry milk over remaining 2 cups water. Beat at low speed on electric mixer. Add corn oil, corn syrup, sugar-gelatin mixture, crushed candy, vanilla and salt. Beat until well mixed. Pour into refrigerator trays or 9 x 5 x 3-inch loaf pan. Freeze until firm about 1-inch from sides of pan. Turn into large bowl and mix well to distribute crushed candy. Return to trays or loaf pan. Cover. Freeze until firm. Seal, label, date. Serve topped with additional crushed candy, if desired. Makes 6 cups.

PEANUT BUTTER ICE CREAM

1 quart vanilla ice cream, softened
1/2 cup creamy or chunk style peanut butter

In large mixing bowl, beat ice cream and peanut butter on low speed of mixer until thoroughly blended, about 2 minutes. Pack in freezer container. Leave head space. Freeze, label, date.

To use: Serve with favorite topping. Makes 1 quart.

LEMON-ORANGE SHERBET

3 cups water	1 envelope unflavored gelatin
1 cup light corn syrup	2/3 cup lemon juice
3/4 cup sugar	1/2 cup orange juice
	1 tablespoon grated lemon rind

Mix together water, corn syrup, sugar and lemon rind in 3-quart saucepan. Cook over medium heat, stirring constantly, until sugar is dissolved and mixture comes to boil. Boil 5 minutes. Remove from heat. Meanwhile, sprinkle gelatin over lemon juice to soften. Add to hot mixture and stir until gelatin is dissolved. Add orange juice. Cool to lukewarm. If desired, strain. Pour into 9x5x3-inch loaf pan and freeze 3 to 4 hours or until mixture is firm. Turn into large chilled bowl. Wash and dry pan to prevent icy layer from forming on bottom. Beat until smooth and fluffy but not melted. Return to loaf pan. Freeze about 3-1/2 hours or until firm. Pack into freezer container. Leave head space. Seal, label, date. Makes 14 (1/2 cup) servings.

FROZEN BANANA POPS

1 (6-ounce) package butterscotch or chocolate chips	1/2 cup creamy or chunk style peanut butter
6 firm medium bananas	Chopped nuts

Melt butterscotch or chocolate chips over low heat, stirring constantly. Stir in peanut butter. Remove from heat. Peel bananas and cut in half crosswise. Insert wooden sticks into cut ends. Dip and roll bananas completely in peanut butter mixture. Sprinkle with nuts. Stand upright in glasses. Place in refrigerator until coating begins to set. Cover and freeze until firm. Label, date.

To use: Remove from freezer 10 to 15 minutes before serving. Makes 12.

Note: Prepared bananas may be frozen before coating. When coated, peanut butter mixture will firm up quickly. Pops can be eaten immediately or returned to freezer for later use.

DESSERT — SALAD

2 6-ounce packages lime or
   strawberry flavor gelatin
4 cups boiling water
2 cups pineapple-peach
   liquid

4 pints uncreamed cottage cheese
2 cans (20-ounce)
   crushed pineapple, drained
2 cans (29-ounce)
   crushed peaches, drained

Line four 8x8-inch pans with freezer wrap leaving enough extra to cover top.

Dissolve gelatin in boiling water. Stir in fruit juice. Chill until mixture begins to thicken. Fold in cheese and fruit. Divide between four pans. Chill until firm. Fold and seal wrap. Label, date, freeze.

To use: Remove from freezer. Unwrap and return to pan in which it was frozen. Defrost overnight in refrigerator. As a dessert serve with whipped cream. As a salad serve on lettuce with mayonnaise. Each pan makes 6 servings.

GINGER MILK SHERBET

1 cup sugar
3 cups milk
1 cup light cream

1 cup chopped preserved ginger
1/2 cup orange juice
4 tablespoons lemon juice

Combine sugar, milk, cream and ginger and simmer ten minutes. Cool. Add remaining ingredients and freeze according to directions with ice cream freezer. When frozen spoon into 2 quart containers.

Seal, label, date and return to freezer.

Storage time: 1 month.

Party Foods

PARTY FOODS

The freezer is a wonderful place to plan a party. Everything, literally, from soup to nuts can be frozen, at the ready for the party day.

How to's With Party Food

- Tray freeze fancy canapes. Then freezer wrap and store in boxes. Serve just defrosted.
- Freeze dips in dishes in which they are to be served. Line dish with freezer wrap having enough extra to fold over top. Fill with dip, freeze. Seal, label, date.
- Freeze meat balls and heat in sauce to serve in a chafing dish.
- Clean, cook shrimp. Freeze, ready to defrost for use when needed.
- Having a cocktail party? Have a frozen casserole ready to heat for stragglers.
- Do not freeze cooked egg whites. They become tough.
- Freeze fruit juice punch in ice cube trays. When frozen remove cubes from trays and store in containers or plastic bags, ready to use to zip up beverages.

Storage Time for Party Foods

Do not plan to store party foods for more than 2 months.

CHICKEN ALMOND FINGERS

2 cups finely diced
    cooked chicken
1/4 cup chopped almonds
1/2 cup mayonnaise

Salt to taste
12 slices thin sliced
    white bread
Butter or margarine

Mix chicken with almonds, mayonnaise and salt to taste. Remove crusts from bread and spread lightly with butter. Spread lightly with filling and cut each slice into 3 finger length pieces. Tray freeze. When frozen, wrap in freezer wrap. Seal, label, date, and store in box in freezer.

To use: Remove from freezer and defrost. If desired, the canapes may be decorated with grated egg yolk, chopped parsley or thinly sliced olives. Makes 36.

SAVORY PASTRIES

1 2-crust package pastry mix
1 can (2-1/2 ounce) deviled ham

2 to 3 tablespoons white wine
Sesame seed

Mix pastry with ham and wine. Roll 1/2-inch thick on a floured board. Cut into small rounds. Sprinkle with sesame seeds. Tray freeze. When frozen wrap, seal, label, date, and store in box in freezer.

To use: Place rounds on a baking sheet. Bake at 450° F. 8 to 10 minutes or until lightly browned. Makes about 3 dozen.

TEXAS SQUARES

1 package (8-ounce) cream cheese	2 teaspoons chili powder
4 tablespoons crumbled	1/4 teaspoon paprika
Roquefort cheese	15 slices bread
2 tablespoons catsup	

Soften cream cheese and blend with Roquefort, catsup, chili powder and paprika. Trim crusts from bread and spread with cream cheese mixture. Cut each slice into 4 squares. Tray freeze. When frozen wrap, seal, label, date, and store in box in freezer.

To use: Remove from freezer and place on broiler tray. Let stand to defrost partially. Broil 3-inches from heat for 4 to 5 minutes or until bubbly. Serve hot. Makes 60 canapes.

SNAPPY CHEESE SPREAD

1/2 pound Roquefort	1/2 teaspoon garlic salt
cheese, crumbled	1/2 cup chopped parlsey
1 cup chili sauce	4 tablespoons
6 tablespoons mayonnaise	finely minced onion

Mix Roquefort cheese with remaining ingredients until well blended. Pack into a 1 pint container. Leave head space. Seal, label, date, freeze.

To use: Defrost in refrigerator overnight. Beat with spoon until fluffy. Serve with crackers. Makes 2 cups.

SHRIMP BALLS

1 pound cooked, cleaned, shrimp
1/2 stalk celery
1/2 green pepper
2 tablespoons cream cheese
1 tablespoon chili sauce

1/2 teaspoon horseradish
1 teaspoon lemon juice
1 tablespoon parsley
1 tablespoon chopped chives

Finely chop shrimp, celery and green pepper in blender. Mix with remaining ingredients. Shape into 30 small balls. Tray freeze. When frozen put into container or plastic bag. Seal, label, date and return to freezer.

To use: Defrost Shrimp Balls in refrigerator. Roll in chopped parsley. Makes 30.

PATE OF SHRIMP

1 pound cooked, cleaned shrimp
3 tablespoons brandy
2 tablespoons lemon juice
1/3 teaspoon Tabasco

1/2 teaspoon salt
1 teaspoon prepared hot mustard
1/2 cup softened butter

Finely chop shrimp in blender. Add remaining ingredients and mix well. Line bowl with freezer wrap leaving extra wrap over edge. Pack in shrimp mixture. Bring extra wrap around and seal. Freeze, label, date. Remove from bowl and return to freezer.

To use: Remove wrappings. Return to bowl in which Pate was frozen and defrost in refrigerator. Makes about 2 cups.

MEAT BALLS WITH CRANBERRY SAUCE

1 pound ground beef	1/8 teaspoon Tabasco
1/2 cup dry bread crumbs	2 tablespoons butter or
1 egg	margarine
3 tablespoons chopped onion	1 cup strained cranberry sauce
1 teaspoon salt	1 can (8-ounce) tomato sauce
	1/2 cup water

Mix ground beef with crumbs, egg, onion, salt and Tabasco. Shape into 25 to 30 small balls. Place on cookie sheet and freeze one hour. Heat butter in skillet and saute meat balls until browned. Add cranberry sauce, tomato sauce and water and simmer about 15 minutes. Cool. Pack into containers. Leave head space. Seal, label, date, freeze.

To use: Defrost meat balls in container in refrigerator. Heat in sauce. Serve in chafing dish or fondue pot. Makes 25 to 30.

JAPANESE CHICKEN BITS

1/2 cup dark corn syrup	3 whole chicken breasts,
1/2 cup soy sauce	skinned, boned and cut
1/4 cup sweet white wine	in bite-size pieces
3/4 cup corn starch	1 pint (approximate) corn oil

Mix corn syrup, soy sauce and wine. Pour over chicken pieces and marinate 1 hour in refrigerator. Drain well on paper towels. Place corn starch in large bag. Add chicken a small amount at a time and shake to coat evenly with corn starch. Pour corn oil into deep skillet to depth of 1/2-inch. Fill utensil no more than 1/3 full. Heat to 350° F. Place coated chicken in hot oil. Fry about 1 minute or until golden. Drain on paper towels and cool. Tray freeze. When frozen, wrap in freezer wrap or pack into a container. Seal, label, date.

To use: Unwrap and heat in a small amount of oil in skillet. Serve hot. Makes about 48 pieces.

CREPES

1/2 cup all purpose flour
1 egg
1 egg yolk
1/8 teaspoon salt

1 teaspoon sugar
1 cup milk
2 tablespoons corn oil

Combine all ingredients in a bowl and beat with a wire whisk until very smooth. Chill several hours in refrigerator.

Oil a 6 or 7-inch skillet and heat over moderate heat. Pour about 2 tablespoons batter into skillet and tilt so that batter covers bottom. Brown on both sides. Remove from skillet and cool on cake rack. Layer crepes with 2 thicknesses of plastic wrap between each crepe. Wrap in freezer wrap. Seal, label, date, freeze.

To use: Defrost crepes. Makes 16 crepes, or 4 servings.

Recipes to use foods from the freezer

CREPES SUZETTE

Blend 1/2 cup soft butter with 1/2 cup sugar, 2 teaspoons grated orange rind, 1/3 cup orange juice and 1 teaspoon lemon juice. Spread on crepes and roll or fold. Put into chafing dish or skillet over low heat. Sprinkle with 2 tablespoons sugar and 2 tablespoons brandy. Warm 1/2 cup brandy. Pour over crepes and ignite with a long tapered match. Serve 4 crepes with sauce for each serving.

CHICKEN CREPES

1 recipe for frozen crepes
1/4 cup butter
1 cup chopped mushrooms
1/4 cup flour
Dash cayenne
1 cup chicken broth
1/2 cup light cream

2 eggs, beaten
2 tablespoons white wine
1/2 teaspoon salt
Freshly ground pepper
2 cups finely minced cooked chicken
3 tablespoons grated Swiss cheese

Defrost crepes.

Heat butter and saute mushrooms until liquid has evaporated. Stir in flour and cook 2 minutes. Add cayenne, chicken broth and stir until mixture boils and is thickened. Mix cream with egg yolks and stir into hot chicken broth. Add wine, salt and pepper. Reserve 1/3 of sauce and mix chicken with remaining sauce. Spoon filling in center of crepes and roll crepe around filling. Arrange in a flat buttered casserole. Pour remaining sauce over filled crepes. Sprinkle with grated Swiss cheese. Bake at 425° F. 15 minutes or until browned and bubbly. Makes 4 servings.

COMPANY CASSEROLE

2 whole chicken breasts	2 tablespoons cornstarch
2 teaspoons salt	2-1/2 cups chicken broth
1 pound shrimp in shell	4 cups cooked rice
1 package (8-ounce)	2 tablespoons chopped parsley
cream cheese	2 tablespoons diced pimiento
1 cup light cream	1/2 cup slivered blanched almonds

Line a 12 x 8-inch baking dish with aluminum foil leaving enough to fold over top of food.

Cover chicken breasts with water, add 1 teaspoon salt and simmer until tender, about 30 minutes. Drain, reserve 2-1/2 cups chicken broth. Remove skin and bones and cut meat into thin slices.

Cook shrimp in boiling water with 1 teaspoon salt about 3 minutes. Drain, remove shells, devein, wash and split crosswise.

Soften cream cheese, blend in cream and beat until smooth. Blend cornstarch and chicken broth and mix with cream cheese mixture. Cook over moderate heat, stirring constantly until thickened.

Spread half of the rice in the bottom of the dish. Arrange half the chicken, shrimp, parsley, pimiento and almonds over the rice. Pour half the sauce over this layer. Repeat with remaining ingredients. Freeze. Cover top with foil, seal, label, date and return to freezer.

To use: Remove wrappings and put food in dish in which it was frozen. Cover and bake at 350° F. for about 1-1/2 hours, or until bubbly. Sprinkle with paprika. Makes 8 servings.

BABA AU RHUM

1 package active dry yeast
1/2 cup lukewarm milk
2 cups all purpose flour
4 eggs, slightly beaten

2/3 cups butter, softened
1/2 teaspoon salt
1 tablespoon sugar

Soften yeast in milk. Combine yeast and flour in a bowl. Add eggs and beat until dough is slightly elastic. Distribute butter over dough and mix it lightly into dough. Cover and let set in a warm place until doubled in bulk. Beat dough again and stir in sugar and salt. Spoon dough into a well greased and floured 2 quart ring mold, or Turk's head mold. Allow to rise until pan is almost full. Bake at 400° F. for 30 minutes or until browned. Remove from pan and cool on rack. Wrap in freezer wrap. Seal, label, date, freeze.

To use: Remove wrappings and return Baba to pan in which it was baked. Cover with foil and heat at 400° F. for 20-25 minutes or until heated through.

Boil together 1/2 cup sugar and 3/4 cup apricot nectar for 10 minutes. Remove from heat and stir in 1 teaspoon lemon juice and 1/4 cup Jamaica rum. Put warm cake on platter and pour syrup carefully over cake so that it soaks in. Just before serving pour 2 tablespoons more rum over cake. Fill center with vanilla ice cream. Makes about 12 servings.

PUNCH FREEZE

1/2 pound mixed dried fruit
Cold water
1/2 cup sugar

3 tablespoons lemon juice
1 cup orange juice
1 cup sweet cider

Wash dried fruit and cover with cold water in a saucepan. Bring to a boil and simmer until tender. Put the fruit through a coarse sieve. Add remaining ingredients and chill. Pour into a 1-quart container. Seal, label, date and freeze.

Storage time: 3 to 4 months.

To use: Defrost. Place in punch bowl with ice cubes. Add 2 quarts carbonated water. Garnish with strawberries. Makes 12-16 servings.

Etcetera

ETCETERA

As was stated in the beginning of this book, almost everything can be frozen. This chapter will take up some of the things that don't fit into other chapters.

- Sandwiches: They freeze very well, but there are a few rules. Always butter the bread to prevent fillings from soaking in. When using mayonnaise in fillings, use commercial mayonnaise. It has less tendency to separate when frozen. Do not put lettuce in sandwiches. Add it after sandwiches are removed from freezer. Do not put tomato slices in sandwiches to be frozen. They become watery on defrosting. Don't plan freezer storage of much more than a month.
- Left-overs: Unless you are very sure that you will use a left-over, do not freeze it. Use it up at once. Left-overs have a tendency to get lost in the freezer and eventually become throw-outs. If you must freeze left-overs, consolidate them in one section of the freezer and make a definite effort to use them.
- Eggs: Egg whites, egg yolks and whole eggs can be frozen. Freeze egg whites as is. Be sure to label the number in the container.

Egg yolks need a little attention. For those to be used for sweet baking, add 3 tablespoons of light corn syrup per cup of egg yolk. Mix well. For other cooking add 2 teaspoons of salt per cup of egg yolks and mix well. Label whether the yolks have syrup or salt, and number of yolks.

Whole eggs should be mixed thoroughly with a fork. Add 1 tablespoon light corn syrup per 2 cups for sweet baking, and 1 teaspoon salt per 2 cups for other cooking. Whole eggs may be frozen in muffin tins or ice cube trays. After eggs are frozen, remove cubes and store in freezer in plastic freezer bags.

Defrost eggs in package. Use egg yolks and whole eggs at once. Egg whites may be stored in refrigerator for 2 or 3 days.

- Butter to freeze should be made from sweet pasteurized cream. Wrap butter in freezer wrap. Seal, label, date, freeze. Salted butter will keep about 6 months, unsalted butter up to 12 months.
- Cheese should be frozen in small pieces as it has a tendency to crumble after defrosting. Use soon after defrosting.
- Approximately 40% butterfat cream can be frozen in liquid tight containers. Leave head space. It stores for 2 to 4 months. Defrost in refrigerator. Use it for whipping. It is not good for table use due to separation.
- Milk can be frozen in its own commercial container or in a freezer container. Storage time is about 1 month. To aid in retaining flavor add 1/4 teaspoon crystalline ascorbic acid to each 5 quarts milk.
- Ice cream, whether commercial or homemade stores well 2 to 3 months. Homemade ice cream using a high percentage of cream and gelatin stores better than a leaner recipe.
- Clean pulp out of orange halves, wash, dry-freeze in plastic bags. Seal, label, date. Use frozen to grate for orange rind.

- All kinds of nuts can be stored in the freezer in containers.
- Freeze small packages of fresh herbs for seasoning off season.
- Make up a roux of flour and butter or margarine and freeze to use as thickening. Label packages as to amount of flour and butter.
- Freezer jams, jellies and relishes save much cooking and retain fresh flavor. The only caution is to store them in the refrigerator after opening.

Recipes to freeze/freezer jams & relishes

FREEZER STRAWBERRY-RHUBARB JAM

1-1/4 cups prepared strawberries (1 pint)	4 cups sugar
1/2 cup ground, unpeeled raw rhubarb (about 1/2 pound)	1 teaspoon finely cut orange rind
	1/2 bottle liquid fruit pectin
	1/4 cup lemon juice

To prepare fruit: Thoroughly wash and remove stems from 1 pint strawberries. Crush and measure 1-1/4 cups in large bowl. Wash, cut off root ends of rhubarb and grind with fine blade. Measure 1/2 cup into bowl with strawberries. Add sugar and orange rind and mix well. Mix liquid pectin with lemon juice in small bowl. Stir into fruit-sugar mixture and continue stirring 3 minutes. Pour at once into sterilized jars and cover at once with tight lids. Leave head space. Let stand at room temperature for 24 hours. Label, date, freeze. Makes about four 1/2-pint jars.

To use: Defrost. After opening, store in refrigerator.

Storage time: Will keep up to 6 months.

FREEZER BLUEBERRY JAM

2 cups prepared blueberries
    (1 quart ripe blueberries)
4 cups granulated sugar
1/2 teaspoon cinnamon

1/8 teaspoon cloves
1/2 bottle liquid fruit pectin
2 tablespoons lemon juice

To prepare fruit: Thoroughly wash and drain 1 quart ripe blueberries. Crush and measure 2 cups into a large bowl. Add sugar and spices and mix well. Mix liquid pectin with lemon juice in small bowl. Stir into fruit-sugar mixture and continue stirring 3 minutes. Pour at once into sterilized jars and cover at once with tight lids. Leave head space. Let stand at room temperature for 24 hours. Label, date, freeze. Makes about 5 1/2-pint jars.

To use: Defrost. After opening, store in refrigerator.
Storage time: Up to 6 months.

FREEZER STRAWBERRY JELLY

1-3/4 cups strawberry juice
  (1-1/2 quarts ripe strawberries)
4 cups granulated sugar

1/2 bottle liquid fruit pectin
2 tablespoons strained lemon juice

To prepare juice: Thoroughly wash and remove stems from 1-1/2 quarts ripe strawberries. Crush berries, a layer at a time and squeeze out juice through a wet jelly bag or cheese cloth in a strainer.

Measure 1-3/4 cups juice into a large bowl. Add sugar and mix well. Mix liquid pectin with lemon juice in a small bowl. Stir into strawberry juice-sugar mixture and continue stirring 3 minutes. Pour at once into sterilized jars and cover at once with tight lids. Leave head space. Let stand at room temperature for 24 hours. Label, date, freeze. Makes about 4 1/2-pint jars.

To use: Defrost. After opening, store in refrigerator.
Storage time: Up to 6 months.

FROZEN CALIFORNIA CRANBERRY RELISH

3 pounds fresh cranberries   3 cups sugar
3 cups pitted fresh dates   1/4 teaspoon salt
3 lemons

Wash and pick over cranberries. Rinse dates and lemons. Cut lemons into halves and remove seeds. Put all fruits through food chopper using medium blade. Mix in sugar and salt, stirring lightly until fruits are blended. Spoon into containers. Leave head space. Label, date, freeze. Makes about 6 pints.

To use: Partially defrost. Store in refrigerator after opening.

Storage time: Up to 6 months.

FROZEN APPLE RELISH

12 tart apples   6 stalks celery
4 green peppers   1-1/2 tablespoons salt
4 sweet peppers   3 cups sugar
1 large onion   1-1/3 cups lemon juice

Wash apples and remove cores. Wash peppers and remove seeds and white ribs. Put apples, peppers, onion and celery through food chopper using medium blade. Mix fruit and vegetables with remaining ingredients, stirring lightly to blend. Spoon into containers. Leave head space. Label, date, freeze. Makes about 6 pints.

To use: Partially defrost. Store in refrigerator after opening.

Storage time: Up to 3 months.

Index